You and Your Deaf Child

You and Your Deaf Child

A Self-Help Guide for Parents of Deaf and Hard of Hearing Children

Second Edition

John W. Adams

Clerc Books
Gallaudet University Press
Washington, D.C.

Clerc Books
An imprint of Gallaudet University Press
Washington, DC 20002

Library of Congress Cataloging-in-Publication Data
Adams, John W., 1956–
     You and your deaf child : a self-help guide for parents of deaf
and hard of hearing children / John W. Adams. — 2nd ed.
          p.   cm.
     Rev. ed. of: You and your hearing-impaired child.
     Includes bibliographical references and index.
     ISBN 1-56368-060-2
     1. Parents of handicapped children—United States.
2. Parenting—United States.   3. Children, Deaf—United States—
Family relationships.   4. Hearing impaired children—United
States—Family relationships.   I. Adams, John W., 1956–   You
and your hearing-impaired child.   II. Title.
     HQ759.913.A33   1997
     649'.1512—dc21   97-18820
                                                                          CIP

Cover design by Dorothy Wachtenheim
Cover illustration by Jeanne Turner
Interior illustrations by Susie Duckworth
Interior design by Alice Fernandes-Brown
Composition by Wilsted & Taylor Publishing Services

∞ The paper used in this publication meets the minimum require-
ments of American National Standard for Information Sciences—
Permanence of Paper for Printed Library Materials, ANSI Z39.48-
1984.

To Cynthia,
Always, John

Contents

Acknowledgments

You and Your Deaf Child is the second edition of *You and Your Hearing-Impaired Child*, which was originally published in 1988. I would like to acknowledge several people who, in many ways, have shared in the creation of this second edition.

To all of the parents of deaf and hard of hearing children who shared their experiences with me and provided their ideas, anecdotes, and inspirations, thank you.

To my friends and colleagues who offered individual and collective understanding and encouragement, your caring and support have sustained me and I deeply appreciate your friendship.

To Pamela Rohring, who served as a consultant for this edition, your first hand knowledge and your experiences as a deaf woman inspired me.

To Ivey Pittle Wallace, my editor, your commitment to quality work and encouragement have made this second effort a successful and worthwhile undertaking.

To my family—Mary Ann, Bill, Mark, Tom, Nancy, and Tina. Your respect and love is a foundation to my persistence. And to my parents—Bill and Mary Adams—your love and guidance established my views of the world and my faith in myself.

And, most especially, to my partner in life, Cynthia. Your intuition concerning others' thoughts and feelings, your knowledge about working with deaf and hard of hearing individuals, your belief in me, your caring ways, and your natural ability to help me grow and learn have enriched my life and the contents of this book.

You and Your Deaf Child

Chapter 1 Introduction

This book is intended for hearing parents of deaf and hard of hearing children. Some of you will be reading this book after you first discover that your child has a hearing loss, others will have experienced the effect of hearing loss on your child and family for years. In any case, this book is about you, your child, and how you interact together. By using this book, you will learn more about yourself and about your child. In reading this book, you have made a commitment to understand more about your child, yourself, and your family. You have made a commitment of caring and of love.

While the following pages can be useful to all parents of deaf and hard of hearing youngsters, those hearing parents having children newly diagnosed with a hearing loss may find the contents particularly helpful. Each of the eleven chapters is designed to provide information of importance to parents of deaf and hard of hearing children. Chapters two and three include material on feelings about hearing loss and a discussion of how to cope with these feelings. Chapter four introduces the topic of family communication and focuses on nonverbal communication. Chapter five continues the discussion of family communication as it relates to family unity. Chapter six involves information about typical child development and how hearing loss and your family's communication system can affect your child's behavior. Chapters seven and eight include material about managing your child's behavior through general limit setting or plans designed to prevent behavior problems. Developing plans for solving future problems is discussed in chapter nine. Presented in chapter ten are general topics of interest regarding hearing loss, such as issues related to technological assistance, choice of appropriate education placement, and an introduction to the Deaf community and culture. There is also a list of resources and suggested readings for parents at the end of the book. You can use these sources to learn more about hearing loss or to obtain help in specific areas of concern.

Chapters two through eight follow a similar format that includes an introductory section that describes the concepts and skills introduced in the chapter; a Skill Development section that reviews the information from the previous chapter and presents the skills and concepts that the reader will learn in the current chapter; a section called Parent and Child that provides interactions and statements that show appropriate use of the skills, principles, and concepts presented; Points to Remember that summarize all the important points of the chapter; and Activities for Practice to hone the skills you have learned.

You are encouraged to read each chapter carefully and to do the Activities for Practice. The Feedback and Answers chapter provides typical responses to the Activities for Practice sections. The length of time it will take you to complete the book depends on many factors—your time, energy, effort, and most important, your understanding about hearing loss and how it affects you and your child. It is important to know that wherever you are at this moment—you are. Take the time necessary to truly grasp and work through the material in each chapter.

Many books are read, put away, and forgotten. *You and Your Deaf Child* is not like other books. You can keep it near, review it, and use it again and again, depending on your needs. In time your thoughts, ideas, and opinions may change. My intent is that parents of deaf and hard of hearing children use the material in this book continuously. In addition to using this book as a reference guide as your child matures, you may also review it based upon your individual needs. You can review particular chapters or combinations of chapters as a source of information. For example, if you experience difficulty in dealing with your feelings or would like to understand feelings related to hearing loss better, you could re-read chapters two and three and complete worksheet 1 in chapter nine. Or, perhaps you would like to understand more about how communication within the family affects each member. Chapters four and five will be helpful to you and then a review of worksheet 3 in chapter nine would be a good idea. If you are interested in learning about typical child behavior at certain ages and how hearing loss influences child behavior and development at different stages, a review of chapter six may be helpful. If you would like to put limits on your child's behavior or want to develop plans for changes toward better behavior in your child, you can refer to chapters seven and eight and complete worksheet 2 in chapter nine. Additional resources for parents of deaf children are in the resource list and in the suggested readings of topics related to hearing loss at the end of the book.

Finally, as you read the following pages, you may need to discuss your reactions and responses to the content with someone else. Parents have used many sources when discussing the material, including friends, family members, other parents of deaf children, deaf adults, and professionals such as clergy, counselors, audiologists, and doctors. It is my hope that you will find *You and Your Deaf Child* helpful, informative, and important in your daily interactions with your child and family.

GUIDELINES FOR USING *YOU AND YOUR DEAF CHILD*

1. *You and Your Deaf Child* is a resource book that parents can use when dealing with feelings about hearing loss and the implications it may have on family life. This book includes various reference materials from primary resources on deafness. The resources include the major areas associated with hearing loss—language systems, family communication, behavior of deaf and hard of hearing children, educational placement, etc. You can seek out information from local, state, regional, and national organizations when help is needed. See appendix 1 for a list of resources.

2. You can go through the book, chapter by chapter, and complete activities at your own pace. If you are unable to complete certain sections of the book or related activities due to difficulties with your emotions or insufficient skill development, this may be a cue that you need to contact various professionals, other parents, or deaf adults and seek support. It is normal for parents to experience various feelings when reading *You and Your Deaf Child*. Most of these feelings are normal and a natural part of everyday living and growth. However, if these feelings are too frequent and of high intensity, it may be important for you to seek additional, outside help.

3. Many parents have found that belonging to a support group of parents with deaf and hard of hearing children to be helpful when using the book. Support groups help parents discover that they are not alone in their experiences and these groups are additional resources during times of need.

4. You are encouraged to read through the book at your own pace. You may skip or skim chapters containing concepts you believe you have mastered, or you may review chapters or concepts within the book you believe to be helpful. Many parents have said that they use the book as an ongoing reference.

5. It is important to remember that the ideas offered in the skill development sections and the activities presented for practice are given only as suggestions. If an idea or an activity doesn't seem to work, it is important not to give up or stop trying. You can seek the perceptions of other professionals, parents, or deaf adults to gain alternative views about your unique family situation.

6. It is important to understand that problems take time to resolve, so results or solutions may not be immediate. *You and Your Deaf Child* may be a first step in the resolution of problems or the prevention of future problems by offering an understanding about how hearing loss affects your life.

<table>
<tr><td>Chapter
2</td><td># Becoming Aware of
Your Feelings</td></tr>
</table>

Learning that your child has a hearing loss can be frightening. Anytime parents experience differences between themselves and their child, uncomfortable feelings may result. It is common for parents to have some difficulty in learning to accept their child's condition. You may be prepared for the diagnosis after making many visits to doctors and from tests you perform at home. But the moment when it is confirmed that your child is deaf triggers feelings and thoughts that are equal to no other.

Following the diagnosis, parents generally experience a wide range of feelings, including sadness, anxiety, confusion, and depression. These feelings are normal, and they are temporary. Although these feelings are natural, they can interfere with the way you interact with your child. This chapter is designed to point out the experiences parents generally have, focusing on the reactions of hearing parents of deaf children.

As you read this chapter and practice the exercises at the end, please try to remember the feelings you had when you first learned of your child's hearing loss. Also make an effort to notice how your feelings influence your interactions with your child. Some of you are still in the process of understanding and adapting to your child's hearing loss. For others, the information provided in this chapter will be a reminder of the past. In either case, it is important that you are aware of when you experience certain feelings and of how these feelings may influence how you and your child interact.

SKILL DEVELOPMENT

Many parents say that they experienced very powerful emotions during the period of time surrounding their child's diagnosis. For example, one parent stated, "We all have expectations for our kids. The first thing that happened after DJ's deafness was diagnosed was that I felt my child had died" (Dolnick 1993). This statement may sound harsh to you. Keep in mind that this parent reacted with an emotional response. Emotions are not rational. Emotions are not guided by our thinking. Therefore, we cannot judge emotional responses as we do our beliefs and the decisions we have made. For hearing parents, having a deaf child involves difficult change and a period of adjustment. Unfortunately, there is no set formula for dealing with such strong emotions. Individuals handle situations differently. The diagnosis of a condition in a child generally brings forth reactions that are similar to those experienced by persons who have lost something of value.

When you lose something that is important to you—such as a loved one, your health, your job, or your dreams of the future—you will naturally experience a period of adapting to change. When adapting to a change brought about by a loss, individuals often express sorrow or grief (Kampfe 1989; Vernon and Andrews 1990). The way you deal with sadness and sorrow usually depends on the way your parents have dealt with loss and on your culture. However, people seem to go through several stages as they deal with a loss. Most parents and professionals agree that parents go through several emotional states or stages when they learn that their child is deaf (Kampfe 1989). Becoming aware of these stages of adapting to loss and learning to recognize what stage you are in, may make it easier for you to cope with these changes.

The Three Stages of Dealing With Loss

Prediagnosis Stage: Awareness and Anticipation

In the prediagnosis stage, the family suspects that something is wrong. The full impact is yet to be felt because the diagnosis has not been confirmed (Goldberg 1979). Many times you feel alone during this stage as you try to convince others that something is different. When you cannot avoid or deny your anxiety any longer, you begin the difficult task of confirming whether or not your child is deaf.

Doctors and professionals often remain distant and say that you are an overanxious parent. Feelings and observations that parents have about their child's hearing loss are often not acknowledged or addressed by doctors, audiologists, and other medical personnel (Beck 1991). These professionals may even say, "Nothing is wrong!" Finally, sometimes after days, weeks, or months of anxiety-provoking visits to doctors or professionals, the words "Your child is deaf" are spoken. Now the painful reality hits. Shock may set in. Many times these words are said in a matter-of-fact, medical manner, as if the diagnosis were one of diabetes. Little is said about how to cope with

the news or how to find more information (Lane, Hoffmeister, and Bahan 1996).

A frequent reason for a delay in diagnosis is that hearing loss is rarely total. Almost all infants can hear a foghorn, pots banging, thunder, or other very loud sounds. They also respond to the vibrations parents make walking across the nursery floor or to the shadow parents may cast across a doorway (Vernon and Andrews 1990; Paul and Jackson 1993). Parents notice that their child sleeps while the vacuum is running, is not startled by some sounds or does not pay attention when someone is speaking. Unfortunately, at times, when parents report these observations to a physician, these observations are seen as common concerns of all parents and not as issues worthy of further discussion or investigation. Also, pediatricians have been known to perform tests in the office that are not much different than those parents have conducted in their homes. The child may be able to visually track the doctor and the child will appear to respond favorably (Lane et al. 1996). It is estimated that in one-third of the cases of childhood hearing loss, misdiagnosis, insensitivity to parent feelings, and ignorance about deafness have occurred. In these cases, a parent's anger with a physician or with other professionals is understandable (Vernon and Andrews 1990).

Diagnosis Stage: Shock and Recognition

The first reaction to the discovery of your child's condition can be shock. Why? Because you now know you have a child who does not fit your expectations. There is a feeling of loss. Shock is a temporary state that passes into anxiety, fear, and often panic. As the initial shock lessens, you may begin to experience strong emotions such as anger, sadness, and possibly, denial (Kampfe 1989). It is common not to want to believe this has happened to you, to your child, or to your family.

You may decide that denial is the best way to cope with your situation or you may use denial unknowingly. Denial serves a distinct and important purpose (Moses 1985)—it helps you cope with danger or difficult times by offering you temporary protection against harm. Denying the condition is a way to avoid the painful feelings and the reality of the diagnosis. You may need time to understand and adapt to what just occurred. You may use denial to buy the time needed to find strength and determine other ways of coping (for example, gathering information, gaining support from friends, developing a sense of belonging through membership in relevant organizations such as parent groups, etc.). But denial is neither constructive nor helpful when you use it continuously to avoid or ignore doing something about your situation. Denial could continue for a few months or a few years, thereby affecting your interactions with your child and, ultimately, your child's self-image.

The following example demonstrates how denial of the hearing loss can be a strong, long-term barrier to constructive action and possibly lead to a child's feelings of lack of acceptance.

> *My mom had trained me to lipread by refusing to write anything when I couldn't understand her. I had to face her and try many, many times until I understood what she said. This was painful at first because I felt they did not accept me for what I [was]. (Okwara 1994, p. 85)*

During the diagnosis stage, it is difficult to make specific plans. Parents experience a broad range of emotions (Scheetz 1993). Both parents may have feelings ranging from guilt about being responsible for their child's condition to sadness about the limitations that they believe the hearing loss will bring.

An important factor in coping during the diagnosis stage is the knowledge of the etiology, or the cause, of deafness. Not knowing the cause of the hearing loss can be a great source of anxiety. This anxiety may affect your attitudes toward and treatment of your child (Meadow 1980). It is, therefore, helpful for you to understand the cause of your child's hearing loss. This knowledge reduces the tendency for you to blame yourself (Mindel and Vernon 1987).

People have several misconceptions about the reasons for hearing loss, ranging from a blow to the head to "brain fever." These typical ideas about the origins of deafness do not offer a true explanation for hearing loss. In reality, there are several different possible causes, any of which could be the very reason for your child's condition. Loss of hearing arises from many causes, some of which are known and others not known. These causes can be from outside of the body (a disease like meningitis, an injury, or drugs) or from inside the body (genetics) (Paul and Jackson 1993). Causes of hearing loss include heredity, blood incompatibility, accidents, drugs, poisons, allergies, bacterial infections (meningitis), viral infections (mumps, rubella, measles), and birth accidents (prematurity, birth injury) (Quigley and Kretschmer 1982; Vernon and Andrews 1990).

Again, knowing the reason for the hearing loss can help you to cope with the situation (Meadow 1968). It can relieve the tension of not knowing what caused your child's condition. It is important to know, however, that for one-third of children who are deaf or hard of hearing, the cause is unknown (Meadow 1980). The unknown category is currently larger than any single known cause of hearing loss (Hardman, Drew, and Egan 1996). Determining the cause of hearing loss is sometimes difficult, particularly because there is often a time lag between the onset of the loss and diagnosis (Vernon and Andrews 1990).

For hearing parents of deaf children, understanding deafness is often a slow and sometimes painful process. More than 90 percent of parents of deaf children are hearing. Most of these hearing parents have never known a deaf person (Higgins and Nash 1987; Ritter-Brinton and Stewart 1992) since deafness is a low incidence condition affecting only a small percentage of the total population (Scheetz 1993).

Unlike hearing parents, parents who are deaf typically do not experience adjustment difficulties when their child is diagnosed with a hearing loss (Paul and Jackson 1993). In fact, deaf parents often prefer having a deaf or hard of hearing child since parents naturally feel more comfortable with a child who can share their same language and culture. Approximately 90 percent of deaf parents have hearing

children (Scheetz 1993; Lane et al. 1996). And they also experience the feelings associated with change and adjustment similar to what you experience as a hearing parent of a deaf child. Having a child that is different from oneself brings about the need for change and adaptation.

Hearing parents not only try to adapt to hearing loss in their family but also to others' expectations, the conflicting opinions of professionals, and controversies about educational methods (Hawkins and Baker-Hawkins 1990). In any case, learning the facts about your child's hearing loss is important. You can shorten the period of your adjustment with accurate knowledge and information.

In summary, during this stage you recognize that your child has a hearing loss. Most hearing parents can relate vividly the exact moment when they realized their child was deaf. They can recount this discovery in emotional detail. They can trace the major changes in their plans for their child and family to those early moments (Higgins and Nash 1987). Not everyone experiences or relives all of the emotions that characterize this stage. A parent's response to his or her child's hearing loss is unique (Ritter-Brinton and Stewart 1992). You may have personally experienced only a few of them. They include sadness, anxiety, anger, guilt, shame, blame, disappointment, hurt, bewilderment, confusion, helplessness, and loneliness. Eventually these uncomfortable feelings decrease in frequency, strength, and the amount of disruption they cause in your life (Hubler 1983).

Postdiagnosis Stage: Recovery and Acceptance

During the postdiagnosis stage, you accept your child's condition. Acceptance does not mean being content with your situation, but it means you are better able to cope with the changes brought to your life. Acceptance of your child's condition does not mean you like it, welcome it, or prefer it. Acceptance means you understand and accept the reality that your child is and always will be deaf (Hubler

1983). Acceptance means that you recognize the hearing loss does make your child's needs different, but your life need not center on this aspect. What you learned during the two earlier stages helps you to deal with your feelings and to adapt to your situation. You are now better able to accept your new role as a parent of a deaf youngster.

Keep in mind that when parents first learn that their child has a hearing loss, they must deal with mass amounts of information, often none of which is understandable. Information regarding hearing loss, its causes, philosophies about educating deaf children, and communication methods may overwhelm you at the same time you are getting to know your child. It is not uncommon for you to feel bombarded with massive amounts of information during the first year of your child's diagnosis (Hawkins and Baker-Hawkins 1990). One piece of information needs to be shared above all, but rarely is—countless numbers of children grow up to become successful deaf and hard of hearing adults (Lane et al. 1996).

Accepting your feelings about hearing loss is a movement toward understanding what is presently happening in your family and a movement toward the future. Feelings are very real when they occur, but they are also temporary. Feelings of pride and accomplishment often replace those of worry and fear (Correspondence Course 1983). For example, as time goes on you may still experience disappointment or fear when your child is attempting something new. However, happy experiences you have had with your child lessen the impact of problematic feelings.

Once you acknowledge the hearing loss, denial and pain will decrease and acceptance will begin. The road to acceptance is not easy. Initially, you may be forced into accepting your child's hearing loss. When the reality of the hearing loss is present, a true adaptation to change begins and the greatest loss is felt (Goldberg 1979). As previously noted, it is very important to remember that you may go through different stages of the change process, and you may use different ways of coping with your feelings than other parents. You may want to discuss and talk through feelings, while another parent may keep feelings inside and find them difficult to discuss. After time, the feeling of crisis fades and healing starts. This period is the beginning of constructive acceptance. Healing starts when you come to know your child as he or she is. At this time, you learn and practice coping behaviors so you can meet your child's needs (Boothroyd 1982).

Feelings are neither good nor bad. They are simply feelings. It may be harmful to pretend that they do not exist. When we ignore feelings such as disappointment, anxiety, rejection, and guilt, troublesome feelings and attitudes can develop (Green 1971). Knowing and accepting that feelings exist is one step you can take to move forward. Being aware of your feelings can help you gain more control over them. Gaining control of your feelings will help give you more energy to do something about your situation.

You may experience frustration from time to time. Being aware of this feeling will help guide you not to act for the wrong reasons. Frustration and sadness may recur in the future. As you and your family grow, you may experience more feelings of loss. The change process is far from being a one-time occurrence. Each time your child comes to a major life milestone, it may affect you in a new way—and you may experience difficult feelings again. With the exception of shock, many difficult feelings may recur during your child's maturation (Mindel and Feldman; Rayson cited in Henggeler, Watson, Whelan, and Malone 1990). For example, you may experience intense emotions when your child begins school for the first time. You may compare your child with hearing children and the differences you discover may make you sad. Experiencing feelings and being aware of them is part of the growth process.

The most subtle challenges may demand adjustment. For instance, listening to other parents discuss their children's academic accomplishments may remind you of the differences between your child and others. Or needing to explain why a particular boy or girl who may not understand hearing loss did not choose your child as a close companion can bring about sadness or even anger.

Many parents experience the feeling that they are different from their children, and this realization is sometimes painful. Parents of hearing children experience this realization slowly as time proves this truth. Hearing parents of deaf children, however, are shown this difference more harshly and abruptly (Kretschmer and Kretschmer 1979). The difference should only be that your child is unique. Your child maintains the uniqueness of his or her own personality and the ability to give and receive love. The main difference between your child and any other is that your child is unable to hear.

Denial and learning the causes of hearing loss were mentioned as ways of coping in the diagnosis phase. You can develop a variety of ways to cope when dealing with the effect of hearing loss on your family's life. Understanding hearing loss and how it influences your child's life and your family structure helps you have hope in the future. The following chapters provide information to aid in your understanding about hearing loss and your child, and can be used to help you cope. For now, let us further discuss helpful ways of coping.

As a human being and a parent, your development is a continuous process. To develop means to change and grow. From time to time, these changes are too sudden, too great, or too unwanted, and you cannot adapt quickly enough (Boothroyd 1982). Having a deaf child presents a time of great change for parents. For example, you as a parent face challenges such as adjusting to your child's condition, developing ways to communicate, trying to understand information related to making appropriate educational decisions, working with a variety of professionals, and purchasing the latest technological equipment (Calderon and Greenberg 1993).

People cope in various ways in order to deal with abrupt changes in their lives. Gathering information and talking to family or friends about the situation are healthy ways of coping. It may be important to get outside support to help with the coping process. Participating in support groups, joining discussions with deaf adults, going to individual and/or family counseling, or visiting clergy available in the community are effective ways to deal with your new situation. For example, parent support groups have traditionally provided a safe place for parents to be honest about their feelings, allowing them to express their vulnerabilities, to discuss their difficulties, and to take pride in their children's accomplishments. Also, understanding hearing loss takes time. It is a process that can be facilitated by interacting with deaf adults (Hawkins and Baker-Hawkins 1990). Additionally, parents have also discovered the importance of taking care of themselves as a way to cope. A refueling process is needed to take care of yourselves as individuals and/or as a couple (Webster-Stratton and Herbert 1994). Refueling can be accomplished through an evening out or a week away from the day-to-day responsibilities of parenting.

It is important to keep in mind that as you develop you will continue to discover new ways of coping. Being aware of your feelings is one way to begin dealing with the changes in your life and in the life of your child. In time, you can use these newfound coping strategies to move ahead, survive, and grow.

PARENT AND CHILD

Listed below are examples of remarks parents have shared regarding the feelings experienced while moving through the stages of grief (partially adapted from Hubler 1983, pp. 5–6):

Shock: "It was a shock to hear about John's deafness—I was stunned."

Denial: "A miracle will happen. There must be a mistake about the diagnosis."

Sadness: "When I hear the birds chirping or a pretty song, I want Suzie to hear it too. We will never be a normal family again!"

Anxiety: "Why did this happen to me? This child will always be a burden."

Guilt: "Did I do something wrong while I was pregnant? How can I make this up to my child?"

Shame: "His father pushes him aside and never wants to do anything for this child."

Happiness: "Now since we have a strong communication system in our home, we share everything as a family."

Blame: "We never expected deafness, I wonder whose fault it is?"

Disappointment: "He will never be the son I wanted him to be."

Hurt: "It hurts; Selma said that her daughter is reading above grade level now."

Bewilderment: "I don't understand what deafness is all about, I don't even know any deaf people!"

Helplessness: "Nothing I can do will make a difference, I feel like giving up."

Loneliness: "Nobody knows what this is like. No one can help."

Acceptance: "Now that I know Tim has a hearing loss, the next step is to find out what it really means."

"Ken is deaf and he is normal in every way—he plays with the dog, is happy to see me and Dad, and is a crazy kind of kid."

POINTS TO REMEMBER

1. The diagnosis of a condition in a child generally brings forth reactions from parents that are similar to those experienced by persons who have lost something of extreme value. When you lose something that is important to you—such as a loved one,

your health, your job, or your dreams of the future—you naturally experience a period of loss requiring change and adaptation.

2. Following the diagnosis of hearing loss, parents often go through stages in which they experience many feelings, including sadness, anxiety, confusion, and depression. Such feelings are normal, and they are temporary.

3. What is important is that you are aware of when you are experiencing certain feelings and of how these feelings may influence the interactions between you and your child.

4. There are three stages of change and adaptation.
   First stage: Prediagnosis. Awareness and anticipation about hearing loss occurs.
   Second stage: Diagnosis. Recognition of the condition. Painful feelings such as anger, sadness, guilt, fear, confusion, and helplessness may surface. Denial should be monitored.
   Third stage: Postdiagnosis. Acceptance of the condition. Acceptance of the new role as a parent of a deaf youngster occurs.

5. Feelings are aroused throughout the prediagnosis (isolation and anxiety), diagnosis (shock, sadness, anger), and postdiagnosis (anger, sadness, despair lessens—acceptance begins) stages for the parents of deaf children.

6. Acceptance of your child's condition does not mean you like it, welcome it, or prefer it. Acceptance means you understand and accept the reality that your child is and always will be deaf.

7. A deaf child maintains the uniqueness of his or her own personality and the ability to give and receive love. The main difference between your child and any other is that your child is unable to hear.

■ Activities For Practice

1. Take two ten-minute periods during the day to observe your child.
   a. Watch your child when her or she is alone. The best time may be during playtime, rest time, or when your child is working. Write down your reactions about what you observe. Be sure to include the feelings you experience as you watch your child.

_____

_____

_____

_____

_____

_____

b. Watch your child interacting with someone else. This may be done when your child is at the dinner table, is playing, etc. The interaction may involve siblings, friends, a parent, etc. Write down your reactions about what you observe. Be sure to include the feelings you experience as you watch the interaction.

_____

_____

_____

_____

_____

_____

2. Take about ten to fifteen minutes in a quiet place to reflect on your reaction when you found out that your child was diagnosed with a hearing loss. Write down the feelings that you experienced. Also write down advice to parents who are in a similar situation. Write this in the form of a letter to yourself as a reminder of what you learned from that experience.

Dear _____,

_____

_____

_____

_____

_____

_____

_____

_____

_____

_____

_____

_____

Sincerely,

_____

3. It is important to understand how you handle grief and loss or other events involving strong feelings. Several different types of feelings are listed below. When these feelings are very strong, how do you handle them? List the ways you usually handle the particular feeling when it occurs.

Feeling	How I Handle This Feeling
depression	_____
anger	_____
loneliness	_____
helplessness	_____
_____ (other)	_____

4. Now that you have written down how you usually handle strong emotions, ask yourself this: Did any of your responses mention expressing these feelings to another person? If not, is there a person with whom you could share your feelings or experiences that cause such feelings? In the space below, list people you can talk with when you are dealing with difficult times, and how they may be contacted. This is your personal support group. Sharing your feelings with another, be it a spouse, friend, clergy, or another parent of a deaf or hard of hearing child, is an important practice for coping with your feelings and experiences. Refer to this list as necessary.

Names in Your Personal Social Support Group

_____

_____

_____

_____

_____

_____

5. Now, rate these individuals with numbers 1 to 5, 1 being the "least helpful" and 5 being the "most helpful." Rate each person according to how helpful they are when you are under little or no stress, and then rate them again according to how helpful they are when you are under stress. The list and the accompanying ratings will help you determine how to use your own personal support group.

Name	Rating Under Little or No Stress	Rating Under Stress
_____	_____	_____
_____	_____	_____
_____	_____	_____
_____	_____	_____
_____	_____	_____
_____	_____	_____

6. Read the sample problem below. Write down how you would handle this situation. What would you tell your child?

Your child, who is about seven years old, comes home and asks, "Why am I different from other kids? Why am I deaf?"

_____

_____

_____

_____

_____

_____

_____

_____

The Future—
Your Reactions and Behaviors

It is important to remember that feelings are normal and temporary. As time goes on, your child may arouse strong feelings within you and others because of his or her special needs and demands. As a human being, you, the parent of a child who has a hearing loss, experience all the feelings other people experience. However, your feelings may be more intense as a result of the emotions you have involving your child's hearing loss and the challenges you face related to your child's condition (Champ-Wilson 1982). The care of your child may include the need for extra supervision, special medical attention, and additional financial costs and considerable involvement with your child's education (Henggeler et al. 1990). Also, you must remember that the adaptation and change process described earlier is not a one-time experience. The feelings associated with your situation are special because their effects continue throughout your life and the life of your family. For example, you may feel you have less time and energy to devote to your own needs and to the needs of other family members (Henggeler et al. 1990). This chapter presents information about how feelings affect behavior. In other words, how you feel determines how you act. Being aware of your feelings as they occur will aid you in determining how best to act with your child as you meet challenging and new experiences in the future.

SKILL DEVELOPMENT

When you first learned of your child's hearing loss you might have experienced the feeling that your world had come to an abrupt end. The hopes and dreams you had for yourself and your child may seemingly have vanished. Life is a series of adjustments. We all continually face new challenges and new information. We eventually learn that when our world suddenly changes, it is possible to adapt to a new one. In doing so, however, we may have to set new goals and have new expectations.

The feelings that you experienced at the moment you discovered you had a child with different needs will often recur. The adaptation

process is repetitive. Strong feelings such as severe anger or even subtle feelings, such as mild sadness, come into being when reality tells you that your child is different from others. Where an irreversible condition is present in a child, the adaptation/change process is open-ended (Paget 1983, p. 79). In most cases, hearing loss is irreversible. From time to time you will be reminded that hearing loss affects your child's life and the lives of your other family members. Throughout your child's life, the condition of having a hearing loss can pose certain limitations on what he or she can do. On the other hand, it can provide different experiences for your child that may bring forth unexpected talents and skills. For instance, your child will be more adept at reading the nonverbal language of family and friends. He or she will be more visually alert to the environment.

At any stage of your life, you may experience some of the same feelings you had when you first discovered your child's hearing loss. For instance, as your child prepares for particularly important events, such as the first days of school, obtaining a driver's license, completing a job application, etc., the effect of your child's condition may again stir feelings of sadness, anger, or frustration within you. When your child wants to play in the neighborhood, the reality of the hearing loss may bring forth feelings of concern for your child's safety or fears that other children may treat your child badly. Again, it is common to experience feelings such as fear, frustration, and renewed sadness when your child faces new challenges and new situations. And, equally important it is also common to experience great happiness, excitement, and contentment when your child reaches new levels of achievement.

Being aware of your feelings can help you be more comfortable with your decisions. To illustrate this point, let's look at the example of your child wanting to play in the neighborhood. Because of the hearing loss, you may want to protect your child from harm or upset and want to keep him or her indoors. Parents naturally want to protect their children from pain, embarrassment, or harm. A parent's

unresolved past feelings can, however, result in overprotection. You may feel guilty about the condition and feel sorry for your child. But overprotection helps only in the short run. In the long run, overprotection is harmful. Young deaf children typically have greater limitations placed on their activities than do hearing children by their parents and by well-intentioned teachers (Marschark and Clark 1993). Overprotection can stifle your child's growth and can present an unrealistic picture of the world. Isolation can result (Calderon and Greenberg 1993). Many deaf adolescents and adults have shared the wish that their parents treat them and their hearing siblings both fairly and equally.

It is important to remember that your feelings are a part of you, but they need not take charge of or control you. Being unaware of your feelings or not knowing what causes them can hinder your ability to make decisions. For instance, on a particular day your child may demand a lot from you and communication may be especially difficult. You may respond by arguing with your spouse when he or she arrives home. The argument happens because you do not acknowledge the frustration you experienced earlier. Your best action might be to discuss the situation and your frustrations with your spouse. Again, feelings that go unchecked can be covered up by new thoughts. However, the feelings do remain and can continue to grow and become more bothersome. Stress can develop from these bothersome feelings. It is natural at times that this stress could significantly affect your marriage, your relationships, and/or your friendships (Greenberg 1990).

To illustrate this point further, let us discuss how family stress can affect your other children. Hearing siblings of deaf children have stated that they felt detached from their families, overlooked, and unimportant at times because of the necessary attention that was devoted to their brothers and sisters (Malcolm 1990). Additionally, hearing siblings have reported being left with the tremendous responsibility of being the primary communicator with their deaf sibling when their parents could not communicate with that brother or sister. When this occurs the hearing sibling can feel overburdened and stressed, and the deaf sibling may feel deprived of real parental contact. One deaf woman reported:

> *I always had difficulty with my hearing sister. I saw her as my mother rather than my sister because she always handled all situations that required serious communication. She was placed in the role of a mother rather than that of a sister. I have resented being cheated of that special relationship.*

On occasion, you and your family will be troubled regardless of the choices you make—whether it be how to handle a problem behavior or where to send your child to school. Never worry over whether you made the "one" right choice. There is never only one right decision. In making decisions, you should first express your feelings and then act on the information you have about your situation (Naiman and Schein 1978).

In order to express your feelings you may need to do something active such as giving yourself time and permission to experience your feelings. Coping with your feelings may also involve shedding tears, taking a nap, or talking with a friend. Having a close family who supports each other has been seen as critical in dealing with life's crises and everyday feelings. Family cohesion (the emotional warmth, closeness, and sharing experienced by family members) is important to a parent's ability to adapt to change and deal with stress (Henggeler et al. 1990). If you do not have close family relationships to depend on, friends, other parents of deaf and hard of hearing children, or professionals could offer you the support you need.

Hearing loss should not obscure your view of your child. You do, however, need to understand the realistic challenges that hearing loss places on your child and your family (Naiman and Schein 1978). Your child's hearing loss will limit the amount of information he or she can receive from spoken language since the auditory channel is not functioning or is limited in its functioning. Because your child cannot receive the same verbal feedback about behavior, feelings, and thoughts that a hearing child can, your child will not fully understand his or her experiences when spoken language is used by itself. Inevitably, if family communication is limited, other differences in behavioral, emotional, and social development may be detected. Many of the social, emotional, and behavioral differences between hearing and deaf children are due to problems in communication

(Adams 1995). The possible causes of behavior problems in deaf children will be discussed further in chapter six.

As time goes on, strong feelings may influence and/or interfere with the way you react to your child's behavior. You may begin to wish that your child were different or were less of a burden. For example, your child, whom you loved as an infant, may be developing into a demanding, difficult person—a stranger with whom you cannot communicate. Also, each new developmental milestone, such as learning to read, may bring with it a return of old feelings and possibly troublesome new feelings. These experiences commonly occur in families such as yours. The problems can be present regardless of the education or financial status of the family.

Feelings cannot be ignored. When you do not express your feelings, situations can become complicated and you may not recognize your true underlying feelings. For example, angry feelings you have about your child's experiences can resurface. If you do not express or acknowledge your anger, you will be a prime candidate for the anger to be turned inward, which can cause depression and guilt. It is only when you ignore your feelings that they may become troublesome. If you are aware of your feelings when they occur, you can use them as powerful coping resources. For example, once recognized, anger can be refocused away from the child and toward your situation. This can bring you closer to acceptance and help you start taking constructive action towards adapting to new challenges and experiences.

Each time you experience feelings you are also given the opportunity to learn. For example, parents often feel helpless and sometimes hopeless in not being able to communicate satisfactorily with their deaf children (Beck 1991). You may have to alter your family goals to adjust to your child's needs, and this change may be unsettling to you and to your family. Your family will need to alter its communication system and perhaps become a bilingual family. Remember, each of these new experiences brings growth. When there is growth, change occurs. When there is change, uncomfortable, difficult feelings or pain can occur as well. Experiencing pain provides the opportunity to develop strength for the future. The difficult feelings you experienced when your child was first diagnosed made you stronger and more prepared to deal with similar feelings in the future. You are better able to solve problems related to these feelings as time passes.

Every major change in the development of your child may demand adjustment. For example, puberty brings about dramatic changes in your child's physical, emotional, and social development.

These changes present parents of all children with dilemmas. But these dilemmas are more complex when a condition affecting communication is present. Explaining the physical changes present in puberty to your child will be more difficult unless clear communication is established. In some cases, the most important stress on parents may be the everyday experience of having a child who is "different" from themselves and who communicates in a different manner (Calderon and Greenberg 1993). A deaf child will have to work harder to learn the English language. This can be an accepted part of the child's life; however, this fact should not prevent parents and others from communicating with the child. A form of communication best suited to the needs of the child and family must be developed early. A lack of an effective communication system in your family will prevent your child and all other family members from reaching their full potential. And, difficulties in communication will add to family stress and make it less likely that difficult feelings will be addressed or resolved. Hearing loss can put realistic obstacles in the path of your family's experiences, but it should not be the focus in preventing your child and family from growing, developing, and sharing happiness.

Many of the feelings you experience are and will be happy ones. You will be able to see the progress you and your child make. Parents who reach a time of acceptance and understanding can begin to take constructive action in their lives. They can laugh at their own vulner-

I marvel at her adjustment to the world she lives in. She plans to do almost all of the things any hearing person would do. Now at the age of 15, she can hardly wait to apply for her driver's license. She's making plans for college and a career.
—Hearing parent of a deaf teenager
(Luterman, cited in Ryan 1992, p. 15)

abilities, express understanding of their child's problems and meet their child's developmental needs. You become an expert at responding to your child's needs and an advocate for your child in the larger community (Webster-Stratton and Herbert 1994). Feelings of sadness and sorrow are replaced with happiness and excitement. When you and your child begin to communicate effectively and your child communicates with other children, your heart will fill with joy. Share these feelings with special others. For these experiences proclaim the truth: Your child is a unique, loving, caring, and special person.

PARENT AND CHILD

Unexpressed feelings can interfere with your daily interactions with your child. Being a parent means you are in a position to make decisions. When you are aware of your feelings, you can make decisions more clearly. Listed below are statements from parents that reflect various levels of awareness of feelings. You can come to your own conclusions as to whether you believe their feelings will negatively or positively affect their actions.

> "I try not to dwell on the hearing loss, my child is a great, good person who is deaf."

> "I am scared to discipline my hard of hearing child like my hearing child; he has been through quite enough already."

> "There's a lot of happiness out there and now we're going to find it!"

> "For my own peace of mind, I've been upset and worried for a long time, I got my child an ID bracelet with her name, address, and phone number. Guess what—now all my children want one, too."

> "I told my husband a joke. We laughed. My son, who is deaf, asked what I was laughing about. I felt so sad. I told him, 'Never mind.'"

> "I know I'm angry at my child now for not looking at me when I'm explaining the situation. Now is not the time to punish him for this. I'm upset and he really doesn't know it."

"My child closes his eyes when he wants to ignore me. I get so frustrated, I slap his hands."

"My child also closes his eyes to ignore me. I know that I get angry. I wait until he opens his eyes and gives me his attention. It takes a while, but by that time I have settled down as well."

Coping With Your Feelings

The following guidelines offer you ways to deal with difficult feelings. Books and other sources that may help you to cope with your feelings are found in appendix 1 and in the Suggested Reading section at the end of this book.

1. Try to recognize the feelings you are experiencing. Make an attempt to name the feelings you are having. They are real and a part of you.

2. When your emotions are high, wait until they subside before you make major decisions. Many times strong emotions can interfere with clear thinking.

3. Encourage members of your family and your friends to discuss their feelings honestly and openly. This can be done through your example.

4. Feelings are neither good nor bad. They are simply feelings. Always remember that everyone has feelings, but there is no one correct way to feel.

5. Talking to other people about the way you feel can help you cope. Feelings can become bottled up inside you. Sharing your feelings with others may help to relieve some of the tension you are experiencing.

6. Talking to other parents of deaf children will be helpful. These parents are experiencing or have experienced feelings and emotions similar to yours. Sharing with other parents of deaf children is important because it shows that you are not alone.

7. Meeting with deaf adults is a great support and resource. You can discuss your questions and concerns about hearing loss, raising a child with a hearing loss, etc. It is also helpful for you and your child to see and interact with deaf role models. Fred Schreiber, a Deaf advocate and role model for many

people, once remarked, "The basic reason for becoming involved with deaf adults [is] we are your children grown. We can, in many instances, tell you the things your child would like to tell you, if he/she had the vocabulary and the experiences to put feelings and needs into words" (Vernon and Andrews 1990, p. 3). Maintaining contact with these adults is a great coping resource.

8. Gather information about hearing loss from a variety of sources: other parents of deaf children, audiology centers, schools with services for deaf children, books, service centers for deaf adults, etc. The more you know about hearing loss, the more you can become aware of the realities of the condition.

9. Continue the plans and routines you have set for you and your family. Discipline, family needs, family activities, etc., need to continue as usual. Your feelings may change from day to day and hour to hour. Being aware of your feelings will help you control the impact they have on your life.

10. You are the best person to choose how to cope with your feelings. Participating in physical exercise, praying, reading, visiting with deaf adults, getting professional assistance, and seeing friends, are different ways people cope with their feelings. Choose or develop the best ways that help you cope.

POINTS TO REMEMBER

1. The adaptation/change process is not a one-time experience. The feelings associated with hearing loss are special because their effects continue throughout your life and the life of your family.

2. An awareness of your feelings can assist you in being more comfortable about decisions.

3. When your feelings are not expressed, situations can become complicated and you may not recognize your true underlying feelings. If you do not express or acknowledge strong feelings, such as anger, you will be a prime candidate for these feelings to be turned inward, which can cause depression and guilt.

4. Feelings such as anger can be refocused away from your child and toward the condition. This can bring you closer to acceptance and help you start taking constructive action towards adapt-

ing to new challenges and experiences. Feelings can be used as powerful coping resources.

5. Your feelings are a part of you but they need not take charge of or control you.

6. In making decisions, you need to express your feelings and act on the information you have about your situation.

7. Your unresolved past feelings can result in overprotection. Overprotection helps only in the short run. In the long run, it is harmful because it stifles your child's growth and presents your child with an unrealistic picture of the world.

8. Feelings cannot be ignored. Each time you experience feelings you are also given the opportunity to learn, which is an opportunity to grow.

9. Many of the feelings you experience can and will be happy ones. Share these feelings with special others. These experiences tell the truth: Your child is a caring, loving person who is deaf.

■ Activities For Practice

1. In the previous chapter's activity, you wrote down ways to handle certain feelings that you experienced. We are now ready to go one step further. Examine some of what you do that eases your mind and helps you relax.

   Physical exercise, prayer, reading, professional assistance, talking to deaf or hard of hearing adults, and visiting friends are different ways that people cope with their feelings. Take a few minutes to write down several activities that calm your feelings and help you cope with a difficult situation.

Feeling   **Coping Activity**

———   ————————————————

———   ————————————————

———   ————————————————

———   ————————————————

———   ————————————————

2. Take ten minutes to think about some of the ways hearing loss affects your life and your child's life. What feelings are associated with these thoughts? Write these thoughts and feelings down. Also, if your feelings are strong ones, write down ways you and your spouse have used to handle these strong feelings.

Ways hearing loss has affected your and your child's life:

_____

_____

_____

_____

_____

_____

Feelings this brings about:

_____

_____

_____

_____

_____

_____

Ways to handle these feelings:

_____

_____

_____

_____

_____

_____

3. Take five minutes to think about how the discovery of hearing loss in your child has made you and other family members stronger or better. If you cannot think of any ways your child's hearing loss has made you stronger, then consider ways it has changed your life. Write down your thoughts in the space below.

   _____

   _____

   _____

   _____

   _____

   _____

4. One way to cope with feelings is to share them with an under-standing person. Some parents of deaf children find it helpful to talk to other parents in a similar situation. If you have not done so already, think of another hearing parent or a deaf parent of a deaf child with whom you can talk. If you have given it some thought, write the name, address, and phone number of this person in the space provided.

   Name of parent of deaf child: _____

   Address: _____

   _____

   Telephone number: _____

5. Other parents of deaf children have found that attending sup-port groups is extremely helpful to cope with feelings and life stress, as well as to share life's greatest joys and accomplish-ments. If you are unsure about whether a support group exists in your area, contact your local school district, Office of Special Education, the school for the deaf nearest to you, or contact the helpline for parents of deaf children at the House Ear Institute: 1-800-352-8888.

6. Some parents enjoy writing in journals about their happy and difficult times. Parents often say that they get a sense of relief by

getting their thoughts and feelings down on paper. Also, many parents enjoy reflecting back on many special, irreplaceable moments. In the space below, write down a recent experience where you and/or your family were happy and write down another time when you and/or your family experienced something difficult. These thoughts provide a starting point for a journal entry.

_____

_____

_____

_____

_____

_____

7. Doing activities as a family to express your feelings will help you, your child, and other family members realize the importance of discussing feelings in order to understand them. Childswork, Childsplay produces games, toys, and feeling charts that can be purchased and put in a "Feeling Box" and stored in your family room. This "Feeling Box" could be used to house family activities that help all members practice understanding and expressing their feelings. You can write the company or call their toll-free number to receive some of their many catalogues.

    Childswork, Childsplay
    Center for Applied Psychology, Inc.
    P.O. Box 1586
    King of Prussia, PA 19406
    (1-800-962-1141)

8. Read the sample problem below. Write down how you would handle this situation.

> You are out with your child at a nearby park. Several neighbors are also at this park. You let your child go to the swings where several other children are playing. These children begin to tease your child by laughing and pointing and saying, "Here's the Deafy."

_____

_____

_____

_____

_____

_____

Communicating Through
Nonverbal Language

When you think of communication, you probably think of speaking, listening, reading, or writing. Our language is, however, both verbal and nonverbal. *Verbal* means any communication that uses symbolic language (spoken, written, or signed language); *nonverbal* means any communication accomplished with gestures or body language (Anderson, Bergan, Landish, and Lewis 1985). We may smile, frown, look angry, or look pleased depending on the situation. Our body communicates nonverbally how we feel and adds to what we are saying. For example, a young baby who is happy and smiling in her mother's arms may begin to cry as soon as the mother lays her down. The child is telling the mother, nonverbally, she would rather be held. Another example is a man standing in a cafeteria line; he is asked by the server if he wants liver and onions. The man gives the server a nasty facial expression and points to the roast beef. The server knows exactly what the man would like to eat even though he has not spoken a single word.

Gestures, facial expressions, and other forms of body language all add meaning to what you communicate. Parents and children use nonverbal language every day to express their wishes and desires. The use of nonverbal language is critical in the lives of all individuals—hearing and nonhearing alike. The parents of deaf children, perhaps even unknowingly, use nonverbal language continually, but they may not be aware that it plays a crucial part in daily communication and in the behavior management of children.

This chapter will help you become aware of the importance of nonverbal language. As you read and complete the exercises provided, you will become better prepared to use nonverbal skills in a purposeful way with your child.

SKILL DEVELOPMENT

The communication process is both verbal and nonverbal (Walters 1989). Our actions, facial expressions, and body movements all communicate to others whether we are listening, enjoying what is happening, or engaging in an activity. Nonverbal language is extremely important as it qualifies verbal language (Cavanagh 1990). Communication is a way of sharing ideas and feelings. A large portion of all human communication is nonverbal. Most people transmit and read body language. For the most part, however, they do it unknowingly (Ogden 1996; Walters 1989). For example, let's say that a man you know is giving a speech to a large audience. Before beginning, he fidgets with materials on the table in front of him, looks through his notes, straightens his tie, and shifts his eyes back and forth. Because you know this individual is competent, you probably dismiss all of these nonverbal cues. Another person attending the same meeting does not know of the speaker's competence. That observer probably will be more aware of the speaker's uncomfortable and nervous behaviors.

Nonverbal language supplements verbal language. In other words, what we do through our actions and expressions adds to what we say—gives extra meaning to it. The use of gestures, facial expressions, and other forms of body language give extra meaning to the verbal response. Nonverbal language is an extremely potent part of communication. In fact, it has been estimated that only 35 percent of the meaning of a social conversation is given by the words actually used (Birdwhistell, as cited in Davis 1973). Some researchers have demonstrated that almost 80 percent of our daily communication is nonverbal (Anderson et al. 1985). Additionally, most people pay more attention to nonverbal language to determine the true meaning of a message (Walters 1989).

Thousands of types of nonverbal behaviors can be listed and discussed (Walters 1989). These behaviors can be placed into three main groups: gestures, facial expressions, and body language. Other individuals may group these nonverbal behaviors differently. And some may put them all in the one category called "body language." Whatever the category or grouping system used, it is apparent that nonverbal behaviors are an extremely important part of communication. These language behaviors with no words or sounds speak volumes about our true thoughts and feelings (*Dateline* 1995).

Gestures

Gestures involve spontaneous movements of the hands, head, or other parts of the body while speaking (McNeill 1993). Gestures help others understand what you are saying and can emphasize the spoken word. This form of nonverbal language can also be used in place of a whole sentence or a paragraph of words. Some examples of gestures are telling a little child it's time for bed simply by putting your head on your hands and pointing to the bedroom, waving hello, holding your hand up to someone talking (which indicates that you've heard enough), and waving your finger to indicate that a behavior was not the correct way to act.

Facial Expressions

Facial expressions add meaning to your words. Your face gives important cues as to your true feelings. Beyond contributing to your

overall appearance, facial expressions serve as a message source to your emotional states of happiness, fear, surprise, sadness, anger, disgust, contempt, or interest. In fact, it has been estimated that our faces are capable of making 250,000 expressions (Ruben 1984).

Often you may be preoccupied or unaware that your facial expression does not match your words or actions. For example, when you are in a store and your child throws a tantrum, you may look around and smile as you tell the child that this is not appropriate behavior (Correspondence Course 1983; Ogden 1996).

Some examples of facial expressions are smiling, frowning, wrinkling the forehead (may indicate worry), pouting, and biting your lip.

Body Language

Body language is a set of nonverbal cues given by the body. These cues support our feelings and words. Body language is considered by many to be the honest form of our communication (*Dateline* 1995). Body language differs from culture to culture, but several types of communication have definite meanings that most people understand or pick up naturally.

Some examples of body language in the American culture are making eye contact (interest or attention), looking at another person but looking away when they return your glance (shyness or keeping distance), blushing (embarrassment), leaning forward when someone is talking (interest), and hanging the head or looking at the ground (sadness or guilt).

Dr. Paul Ogden, a profoundly deaf professional, has related the following experience from his childhood. The story represents the usefulness and the complexity of nonverbal language:

> *When I was about twelve years old, my brother took me to the airport to meet our parents on an incoming flight. While waiting for the plane, we sat across from a row of doorless telephone booths, all occupied. As I scanned the line of people talking on the phones, I could tell which ones were enjoying their conversations and which were not, which were talking with people they liked or loved and which with strangers or business associates, which were nervous about what they were saying and which were talking naturally. I could even speculate about who was lying or telling the truth (Ogden 1996, pp. 95, 98).*

How much more could a person have learned without listening to the actual conversations of these people? The use of nonverbal language is a way of sharing information and feelings. But as Ogden's story illustrates, nonverbal language can tell you much more than verbal language alone. Nonverbal language adds meaning and verifies what you say and do. Hearing loss affects hearing and speech but not the ability to communicate. Deaf children have their hands, arms, faces, eyes, and bodies with which to communicate (Ogden 1996). Communication is a natural impulse for any human being.

Using nonverbal language to communicate is a natural part of child development. For example, between the ages of 14 and 24 months, a child is able to express affection for people. The child can show jealousy and joy through contact movements such as poking, hitting, and caressing—all of which are nonverbal means of language (Ruben 1984). As children grow, they display a natural ability for nonverbal language. Deaf children are no exception. When interactions with a deaf child involve oral language only and nonverbal language is disregarded, the possibility of actually experiencing a meaningful interaction with the child is reduced. Nonverbal language should be viewed as a deaf child's innate talent to express him or herself. Research has shown that babies who have been exposed to purposeful nonverbal language at an early age have shown growth in language development. This does not mean that nonverbal language

should be used instead of verbal or spoken language for some deaf children. Nonverbal language supplements and enhances these forms of communication. A deaf child tunes in early to your facial expressions, your body movements, and the cues given by your eyes.

It is just as important for you to cue into your child's nonverbal language as it is for you to practice your own nonverbal language skills. Cuing into your child's nonverbal language will give you a better understanding of your child's behavior. Consider the following example:

A deaf three-year-old boy is playing with his favorite truck and puts it away in the closet. Two days later he wants to play with his truck but cannot remember where he put it. His mother is ironing in the other room. The little boy runs up to his mother frantically gesturing for her to come and help him look for the truck. The mother asks the boy clearly, "What do you want?" The boy, in tears, continues to gesture to the playroom but is unable to communicate effectively that he has lost his truck. The mother, thinking that the boy wants to play, tells him to go ahead and play; she points to the room and nods her head. The boy, now frustrated, bursts into tears, and throws a temper tantrum, for which the mother punishes him and sends him to his room.

This story gives an example of what can happen when a parent does not tune into the nonverbal cues of her child. The mother picks up only on the boy's insistent pointing behavior to the playroom and does not pick up on his worrisome looks and his shrugging shoulders. The boy's nonverbal behavior is a sign of his losing something rather than a request to do something. Remember to cue into the nonverbal language of your child to understand the message being communicated.

Just as your child's nonverbal cues are important, the nonverbal language you use is extremely important to your child. Your facial expressions, body movements, and eye contact are all pieces of meaningful information to your child. Do not hold back these important sources of information. Holding back can only hinder your child in accurately receiving your verbal messages.

Deaf children need all the visual cues available to clearly receive your messages. For example, eye movements can communicate excitement, pain, happiness, sadness, and doubt. Maintaining eye contact provides the visual cues necessary for your child to understand the tone of your voice (which is available to hearing people). The eyes can communicate your mood to an individual aware of nonverbal cues (Ogden 1996). Inhibiting yourself from using gestures, body movements, and eye contact will prevent your child from getting to know you and from understanding your messages. Parents who have both hearing and deaf children often are more expressive with their hearing children (Correspondence Course 1983; Ogden 1996). Remember to be naturally expressive with all of your children. If the content of this chapter helps you become more aware of the importance of nonverbal language in the lives of all children, it has accomplished its task.

Using nonverbal language is a technique that gives clarity to what you say or do, and also helps you develop consistency as a behavior manager and a clear communicator. Your ultimate goal is to send a clear, consistent message that cannot be misinterpreted by your child. Awareness of nonverbal cues can help you in this goal.

Consistency is an important area of concern for parents of deaf children, since confusion is inevitable when the body and the intended message contradict each other. When you are not in total control of your body (when you feel tired or apathetic), your body movements can be inconsistent with the message you are trying to convey. Remember that your child is well-versed in the meanings of your expressions, gestures, and postures. When you are tense and feeling uneasy, your child looks beyond your smile and notices the feelings in your eyes and facial expressions. Since the deaf child is in tune with your nonverbal methods of communication, you must back up your words with meaningful nonverbal, visual cues.

For deaf children, communication is visual, different from that of their hearing parents (Greenberg 1990). Deaf individuals must receive information through their eyes. When communicating with your deaf child, you may feel exasperated since you are not accustomed to communicating within a visual framework (Trychin 1990). Deaf children need to visually attend to all of the communication that happens and also to what is happening in their environment. Hearing children can visually pay attention to the environment and simultaneously hear speech (Lederberg 1993). Visual attention and visual aspects of communication are vital to deaf children to obtain meaning from their world. Even young deaf babies scan their environment more often than hearing babies. They look around for visual cues so much that they spend less time focusing on their toys than do hearing children (McConnell 1996). On the other hand, maintaining visual attention and being visually alert is difficult for hearing parents who use a spoken, auditory way of communicating. Being more visually attentive to communication will help you practice critical nonverbal language skills. In the past, parents and professionals believed that focusing on children's nonverbal and visual language needs would result in their having difficulty developing oral language. Controlled research studies conducted by the National Institutes of Health, show that focusing on *any* child's nonverbal and visual language needs early in life, actually facilitates language development (*Today* 1996). Using visual aspects of language will be discussed further in chapter five.

Guidelines for Use of Nonverbal Behaviors

1. Stay calm. Be careful not to scream, yell, or force your requests. By staying calm, you communicate to your child that you are in control.

2. Look your child in the eyes when you speak. Eye contact is important to human communication. We say as much with our eyes as with our words. You can increase the effectiveness of your messages with eye contact.

3. Emphasize your words with gestures. Hand gestures often communicate nonverbally to the child, "I mean what I'm saying." Remember, however, that there is a difference between a hand gesture designed to emphasize your words and one used to intimidate your child (e.g., shaking your finger in your child's face).

4. Touch your child. Touch creates a physical as well as verbal limit. As you speak, gently place your hand on your child as a clear indication of your caring and your sincerity.

(Adapted from Canter and Canter 1985, pp. 17–18.)

Nonverbal Language and Discipline

Both adults and children use nonverbal language to express themselves. Children have a natural talent for nonverbal language (Ogden 1996). In their little world, they roam about seeking boundaries through their senses. They look, listen, touch, taste, and smell to learn about their environment.

Children tune into our facial expressions and gestures at an early age. It is important to understand the power of nonverbal language as you interact within your family. Using nonverbal language is a powerful tool when you try to teach your children the proper ways of behaving. Discipline is a communication process and using nonverbal aspects of communication is a vital part of that process. Often, nonverbal communication with your child can be a subtle process. Parents of deaf children need to analyze their nonverbal language to determine the effectiveness of their communication in conveying their intended meaning. The following example will illustrate this point:

A six-year-old deaf girl was sitting at the table waiting for her lunch. Her mother wanted to heat her daughter's spaghetti in the microwave so that she could begin to eat as soon as possible. The six-year-old began to tug at her mother's shirt sleeve and point to her plate. The mother tried to display a facial expression that would tell the child that she needed to be patient because the food was going to be put in the microwave. Instead, the facial expression came across like a frown and the mother nervously moved her daughter to her seat at the table. The six-year-old began to cry and ran from the room (Winslow 1994).

In the above example, the child's mother was unaware that her facial expression (nervous frown) did not match the meaning of her message (please wait). The child, adept at reading nonverbal messages, assumed that her mother was cross with her. You may sometimes be unaware that your body movements or facial expressions are inconsistent with the message you are trying to convey. It is important for parents of deaf children to think about the nonverbal and visual messages they wish to send their children so their communications are clear and cannot be misinterpreted. Also, some feelings are harder to convey than others. Think about how you would display disappointment and sadness without using words. Since these two feelings are expressed in somewhat similar ways on the face, you will need to be sure that your child recognizes the differences of these feelings through your nonverbal language. Observing how you communicate these feelings through your facial expressions may help you to explicitly display them to your child.

Proper use of nonverbal techniques helps add consistency to

Techniques to Enhance the Effectiveness of Nonverbal Language

There are specific techniques that can help you clearly communicate your nonverbal messages to your child.

1. Communicate with your child at eye level. Kneeling down will enable you to make direct eye contact with your child.

2. Eye cues give subtle meanings to your verbal messages. Stay aware of your head movements in order to make it easy for your child to see your eyes.

3. Be as responsive as possible with your face and body to all of your child's messages. The deaf child needs nonverbal cues from you to indicate that you are listening and understanding.

4. Use gestures as much as possible, and make your gestures as normal as possible. Many gestures are universal and can be understood by your child.

5. Refine your body language as your child gets older. The older the child, the more subtle and complex the cues become.

(Adapted from Ogden 1996, pp. 94–95.)

your discipline. If you use appropriate nonverbal behaviors with your verbal language, you will send clear, consistent messages that cannot be misinterpreted. For example, suppose your child comes up to you during an important dinner party gathering and asks to go outside. You politely say no and point to the play area and nod your approval. Your child goes to the play area and begins to make a tremendous amount of noise. You go to your child and communicate that the noise is not appropriate. In front of your friends you are a bit nervous, yet you look sternly at your child and say, "Stop." Your child picks up that your facial expression and your body language are giving firm support to your words. Your child stops making noise.

If you had smiled nervously and communicated *stop* to your child, then he or she may have read your nervous smile as a *go* sign for making noise. Remember that your child does not understand that you would be embarrassed or that you would try to save face. Your child would simply read your nonverbal cues in addition to your spoken words. Children attend to the information that they think ex-

Nonverbal Language	Verbal Language Equivalent
Look very displeased and shake head from side to side. Be very firm and rigid in your facial expressions and posture. Touch child, act out the misbehavior if necessary and again firmly shake your head from side to side.	"No! That is not acceptable."
Point to the child with a questioning look on face. Shrug your shoulders and point to activity in question.	"What are you doing?"
Show a worried look on your face with a questioning expression. Point to child. Touch the child to show you care while using a questioning expression.	"What is wrong?"
Smile and look pleased. Touch the child and point to what he or she has done to please you. Act out behavior if necessary. Let your whole body, arms, shoulders, face, etc., show your happiness.	"Good job, well done!"
Show or act out options. Use a questioning expression. Point to both choices and then to the child.	"Which do you want?"

plains the meaning of the words, that is, the nonverbal behaviors of their parents. You must practice using nonverbal behaviors in order to send clear and consistent messages to your child.

And finally, using nonverbal praise is extremely important in your interactions with your child. A hug, smile, wink, or a pat on the back can all communicate more than several "goods" or "nice jobs." These nonverbal behaviors all let your child know that you support and recognize his or her appropriate behaviors.

PARENT AND CHILD

When you use nonverbal language, you let your child know what you mean through the use of your eyes, facial expressions, and body movements. The examples listed on page 43 (adapted from Ogden 1996, pp. 96–98; Walters 1989) demonstrate that using nonverbal language is a very powerful tool for behavior management as well as in everyday conversation.

POINTS TO REMEMBER

1. When you think of communication, you probably think of speaking, listening, reading, and writing. Our language is, however, both verbal (involving spoken, written, or signed language) and nonverbal (involving gestures, body language, facial expressions, etc.).

2. Gestures, facial expressions, and other forms of body language all add meaning to what you communicate. The use of nonverbal language is critical in the lives of all individuals—hearing and non-hearing alike.

3. Nonverbal language supplements verbal language. In other words, what we do through our actions and expressions gives meaning to what we say.

4. Children have a natural ability for nonverbal language. Children often learn and express themselves through nonverbal language.

5. Nonverbal behaviors can help parents send clear and consistent messages to children.

6. Nonverbal praise is extremely important in interactions with children. A hug, smile, a wink—all lct your child know that you support and recognize his or her appropriate behaviors.

7. Nonverbal language should be viewed as a deaf child's innate talent for self-expression.

8. Nonverbal language is not used instead of speech or verbal language; it supplements these forms of communication.

9. Your facial expressions, body movements, and eye contact are important sources of visual information to your deaf child. Do not hold back these important sources of visual information.

■ Activities For Practice

1. Think about greeting a friend that you haven't seen for ten years without using nonverbal body language. Write down your comments about the picture you have in your mind. Consider this: If you only use your voice, the old friend may receive your message as a snub or an unenthusiastic greeting.

   _____

   _____

   _____

   _____

   _____

2. Spend time in front of the mirror to determine what messages you are sending to others. Use the chart on the following page to see what gestures and expressions you would use to match the message you wish to convey. Look at yourself in front of the mirror as you act out these nonverbal behaviors. This may seem a little embarrassing to you at first, but it will give you an idea of how important nonverbal messages can be. This activity is not used to teach you how to create nonverbal messages but to help you to become aware of how you already use them. Write your comments in the chart.

Nonverbal Behavior	Comments
Example: Show that you are sad.	I made a sad face in front of the mirror and checked to be sure that my child would understand my expression clearly. I lowered my head and made an exaggerated frown with my mouth.
a. Show that you are very pleased.	
b. Show that you are trying to figure out a complex problem.	
c. Show that you are worried about the outcome of a situation.	
d. Show that you are firm and consistent about a rule you have set for your child.	

3. During one day this week, choose thirty minutes to watch people around you. This can be done during a lunch break from the office or on your way to church, in a restaurant, etc. Observe the nonverbal language taking place during several different interactions. Note if the individuals seem happy, sad, bored, etc. Make mental notes about all of the forms of nonverbal language you observe. After you observe for half an hour, take five minutes to write down your observations.

_____

_____

_____

_____

_____

_____

_____

_____

4. Review the techniques about communicating your nonverbal messages. Choose a variety of situations during which you will actively use these techniques with your child. Write down the techniques you used and their results.

Example: When I told Susie that she couldn't have a cookie before dinner, I shook my head no and pointed to the cookie jar to show her that she had to put the cookie back inside. Susie seemed to understand this better than in the past when I would just said no or when I would take the cookie away from her.

_____

_____

_____

_____

_____

_____

_____

_____

5. Read the sample problem below. What do you think was the reason for Mary's behavior?

Mary is twelve years old and has a mild hearing loss. She occasionally likes to turn up the volume of the stereo in the dining room to hear some of her music tapes. Mary's mother is entertaining business guests in the den located two rooms away from the dining area. Mary turns up the stereo when she arrives home from school. Mary's mother and her business associates are startled and come into the dining room.

Mary's mother, embarrassed and smiling, tells her daughter to turn down the music a little bit. One of the mother's business partners say, "Oh, isn't she sweet!" They return to the den. Minutes later, Mary turns up the volume on the stereo even louder.

_____

_____

_____

_____

_____

_____

_____

_____

Chapter	**Promoting Family Unity**
5	**Through Communication**

Let us begin this chapter by defining what is meant by the term *unity*. Unity implies harmony among parts to form a whole—the condition of many, becoming one. Family unity requires that each member of the family contribute to the family unit without losing his or her identity. Parents, as head of the family, are indeed important in the development of the family. However, each family member is key in maintaining the unit's harmony. Each child contributes his or her personality, wishes, and desires to add structure to the family unit just as a variety of colors, textures, and forms harmonize and provide structure to a beautiful landscape painting.

Parents of deaf children encounter a unique challenge to family unity. Since most of these parents are themselves hearing, they experience the feeling of being different from their child. As stated in chapter three, some parents have said that the child who they expected to be very much like them became a stranger with whom they had little in common after the diagnosis of hearing loss. The hearing loss in their child was a real difference that seemed to set them apart. Their deaf child became the focus of the family unit rather than an active member in it. This can happen regardless of how well prepared parents may feel.

For example, a pediatrician and a school teacher, both hearing parents of a deaf two-year-old, believed that they could quickly adjust to their child's hearing loss. However, they discovered that they were often at a loss as to what to do and their day-to-day experiences shook the family's very foundation.

The fact that hearing parents and deaf children do not experience the world in the same way demands adjustment in the family system (Henderson and Hendershott 1992). Hearing parents need to make adjustments in their family unit to include a child who has a hearing loss and thus experiences the world differently from them. Dealing with feelings, understanding child development and behavior, and creating a family communication system are critical steps for a family whose goal is unity. I. King Jordan, President of Gallaudet University, states that communication in the family is critical in influencing the future of deaf and hard of hearing children (Weiss 1994). This chapter will present information about family communication as it affects family unity. Given the amount of information presented in this chapter, the Parent and Child section is abbreviated.

SKILL DEVELOPMENT

Will my child learn to talk? This is often a first question asked by parents of deaf children (Plapinger and Kretschmer 1991). Deaf youngsters nearly always experience English language delays or deficits (Schlesinger 1985). Many different factors can influence a deaf child's English language development. The child's age at the onset of hearing loss and the amount of residual hearing, and the hearing status of the parents are among the various factors. Like all children, deaf children have a capacity for language, which may or may not include spoken words (Mindel and Vernon 1987). In fact, research indicates that hearing loss and the use of speech are incidental to the learning of language (Arieff 1991).

In order for language to develop, you must actively seek out communication interactions with your child. These interactions can occur during such routines as getting ready for school, playtime, games, dinner, and bedtime. For example, you can use activities such as lunchtime, bathtime, or getting dressed to encourage your children to talk about past events familiar to them or about what may happen in the future. And, you can use activities such as playtime to talk about what is happening at the moment for language practice (Plapinger and Kretschmer 1991). Through play, natural conversation happens. Play activities provide the foundation for literacy and overall language development (Goldberg 1995). You must be actively involved in helping your child refer to the world in a meaningful way. The development of effective language is connected to the availability of interactions you provide (Heimgartner 1982).

Characteristics of family members influence family unity in different ways. Hearing loss is a condition that changes the family's overall communication system and the entire structure in the home. For example, once a child is diagnosed as deaf, the family unit is no longer considered *hearing*; the parents may be hearing, the other children may be hearing, but the family unit becomes *hearing and deaf* (Henderson and Hendershott 1992).

Within this new family unit, the problem is not that deaf children are being deprived of sounds as much as they are being deprived of language and communication (Meadow 1980). Being deaf per se does

not lead to problems in communication; deaf parents communicate quite well with their deaf children (Sloman, Perry, and Frankenburg 1987). For example, deaf babies of deaf parents babble with their hands just as hearing infants babble through their speech. It appears that deaf infants learn the motions of the hands by watching their deaf parents communicate through sign language.

Good communication patterns established early in the home have been related consistently with positive child development (Garbarino 1992; Nowell and Marshak 1994). Communication affects every aspect of our human development from dealing with feelings to managing behaviors and discussing our culture. Communication is critical in our lives and in the lives of our children. The development of an optimal communication system between parents and children is critical in the emotional development of deaf children (Stinson 1991). Your child will have difficulty communicating wants, needs, thoughts, and feelings if a strong communication base is not established early in the home.

The single largest issue facing parents in maintaining a family unit is the task of involving all family members in communication in the home. As stated before, a primary source of stress for hearing parents is the experience of having a child who is "different" and needs to communicate in a different manner (Calderon and Greenberg 1993). Deaf children *see* communication and hearing children *hear* communication. For this reason, above all, the family environment for deaf and hard of hearing children must be visual (Bravin and Bravin 1992).

Research has shown that deaf children with deaf parents, who share a common language and communication system, have an advantage when attempting a variety of life's tasks (Paul and Quigley 1990; Ritter-Brinton and Stewart 1992). Deaf parents are resources to all parents of deaf children. They should be considered experts in communication with deaf children. Many professionals in deaf education believe that the lags in academic achievement that deaf and hard of hearing children experience in school are related to deficits in early communication within the majority of hearing families (Poor 1992). Most deaf children of deaf parents function better than deaf children of hearing parents in all academic, language, and social areas (Lane et al. 1996).

Communication in the family creates the bond that supports the structure of the family unit. Hence, communication is the backbone of a strong family structure. When communication is inadequate, the outlets for venting frustration and working through difficult situations, as well as celebrating happy moments or subtle enjoyments, are often limited. For example, one deaf adult stated that the communication between her and her parents was almost nonexistent. It was based solely on rudimentary gestures indicating *sleep, eat, yes, no* (Sevigny-Skyer 1990). This scenario is *not* uncommon; it can be heard from many deaf and hard of hearing youth. In the absence of a shared communication system, a general sense of isolation among family members can exist (Kluwin and Gaustad 1992).

If you think back on some of your most enjoyable moments as a child, you may remember a trip to Grandma and Grandpa's house where you listened to them describe their past life experiences. Or, you may remember sitting around your own family dinner table where, during a meal, you discussed important things that happened to you on a particular school day. Or, you might recall Sunday trips by car to the local ice cream parlor where you anticipated telling your parents your favorite flavor of the day. Each one of these scenarios involves family conversation, an important part of the family communication system.

Most children first experience and learn language through conversation with family members. Throughout childhood, as we learn to become competent, independent communicators, we use family conversations as a practice field. We use conversation to try out new language skills and new ideas and as a foundation to develop our relationships (Bodner-Johnson 1988). Family conversation is an important vehicle for developing intellectual and social skills, and for developing a sense of belonging to the family unit (Turnbull and Turnbull, cited in Bodner-Johnson 1991). Dialogue between adults and children influences a child's progress in language, intellectual, and social abilities. Dialoguing is the conversation exchange of information between two or more people. According to Vygotsky (who wrote extensively about language development), a child's language development and eventually his or her intellectual development is enhanced when the child is involved in social interaction. Dialoguing stimulates language and intellectual growth and leads to independence and self-control in each individual (cited in Scheetz 1993).

Hearing parents tend to use more directive statements with their deaf children than with their hearing children (Jamieson 1994). Jamieson found that hearing parents told their deaf children what to do, but rarely discussed what was expected of them. In another study, mothers of deaf children were seen to initiate topics and direct the interaction toward what the parent saw as important instead of following the child's lead (Plapinger and Kretschmer 1991). Some parents of deaf children have stated that they often feel they are teachers and not parents. Parents in the role of teachers have limited time for dialoguing with their children. Perhaps parents fall into this teaching role and become more directive in their style of interaction because of problems in family communication. Parents may believe they need to teach their child aspects of language constantly so their child can succeed in developing communication skills.

Establishing a Communication System Early in Family Life

Establishing a family communication system that is followed consistently is critical to strengthening the family unit. Early communication difficulties between hearing parents and their deaf child impede future interaction. If your child has limited participation in your family's interaction, he or she is at risk for restricted access to family life (Bodner-Johnson 1991). Your child is an important part of your family's structure. If your child is separated, left out, or ignored while the family communicates—isolation will occur. Consider the plight of a deaf adolescent who saw the light flashing indicating a phone call. Her grandmother spoke on the phone for several moments and was unable to tell her granddaughter who had called and that the phone call was not for her. She was unable to tell her due to her own lack of communication skills. Siblings of deaf and hard of hearing children report that they turn to others outside the family for close relationships because they are unable to communicate with deaf or hard of hearing brothers and sisters (Kluwin and Gaustad 1992). Deaf children need to be included in family conversations and dialogues as important members of the interactions. Only when the deaf child is accepted as an equal participant in the family unit, will the family be able to provide the full range of support that the child needs (Henderson and Hendershott 1992).

Parents may act differently with their deaf children than they do

with their hearing children. This situation can alter family functioning and affect the child's future interactions. The following story provides a good example of how family interactions affect one's life.

> *One day while having lunch with a friend, a deaf man ate
> quickly looking up only on occasion. His friend asked if he
> were eating quickly so he would have time to relax and chat
> after lunch. The deaf man commented that when he was grow-
> ing up as a boy, dinner time was not important. He explained
> that his family carried on spoken conversations in which he
> could not participate. And, although he tried to become part
> of these conversations by visually attending and speechreading,
> he still could not follow them. After awhile, he learned to with-
> draw from the interactions that did not include him. Eating his
> meals quickly helped him to avoid frustration.*

As the story indicates, the man's early interactions taught him
that family dinner was not the time for dialogue, conversation, and
the exchange of information, but a time of confusion and exclusion.
Unfortunately, this deaf man's experience is typical of what is experienced by many deaf children raised in families with hearing members. Dinnertime should be an opportunity for family conversation,
which is found to be significant in establishing family unity. Setting
up a communication system in your home early will enable all members to participate equally in family conversation such as that found
at the dinner table.

Another deaf adult tells the following story:

> *I was born deaf of deaf parents who also had an older deaf
> son. Therefore, my family was entirely deaf, and we lived in a
> world of our own. I grew up in a loving atmosphere and never
> knew any deprivation of communication. My parents knew my
> wants, and I knew just how far I could go without bringing
> their wrath down on my head. The conversation was full and
> interesting at the dinner table.*

Besides interactive conversation, it is important for parents to
provide activities in the home in which all members can participate
and contribute—making a family meal, developing a family scrapbook, watching captioned television, etc. For example, storytelling is
an excellent way for children to develop language since it provides a
meaningful opportunity for interaction (Schick and Gale 1995). All

children need to be included in family activities on a daily basis to experience a sense of belonging, love, security, and family unity. One family uses the following technique:

We all sit down at the dinner table to eat. After the portions are served, each child shares with the family something important from their day. Each of us passes a "communication spoon" around the table and no one is allowed to communicate until the "communication spoon" is in his or her hand. Since Donnie can't hear, the "communication spoon" helps him visually follow the conversation at the table. This method has helped all of us pay closer attention to who is communicating and is also lots of fun!

Early Communication: Some Choices

Good communication involves much more than just an exchange of words. Communication implies an interaction that involves sharing. It is important that a family with a deaf member use an easy, fluent system of communication that all members of the family can understand (Quigley and Kretschmer 1982). There exists little disagreement about the need for an easy, fluent communication system; the disagreement comes in choosing the types of communication methods and language to be used. The communication issue is considered the most controversial issue related to hearing loss (Moores 1987; Paul and Jackson 1993; Paul and Quigley 1990).

The best method of communication for deaf children has been hotly debated for years. The conflict has focused primarily on the use of spoken language versus sign language (Meadow 1980). The choice of the method of communication used with your child is yours and yours alone. Your choice should be made after carefully considering what is best for your child and for your family. It all relates to parents making decisions for their children and making them early (Goldberg 1995).

The following paragraphs contain information about a few of the options available to parents regarding their choice for communication method. Given that these methods have been debated for more than one hundred years, vast amounts of information are available discussing the merits of each method. Please see the resource list, the list of suggested readings, and the reference section at the end of the book to find more information about each of these communication choices. The information presented below is for definition purposes only.

Oral/Aural Method

Individuals promoting the oral/aural communication method stress the use of speech, hearing aids, voice, and speechreading skills. Children using this method are discouraged from relying on visual cues except those involved with the lip movements used in speech. Proponents of this method promote the teaching of oral communication skills and the training of residual hearing to facilitate language and speech development (Becker 1981). One of the primary objectives of this approach is to develop intelligible speech (Scheetz 1993) and age-appropriate oral language (Connor, cited in Paul and Jackson 1993). In the traditional oral approach, early amplification, auditory training and/or oral language learning activities, speech training, and parental involvement are critical features (Paul and Jackson 1993). The ultimate goal of this method is to provide the child with oral skills that will enable him or her to function in a hearing society (Goldberg 1995).

Cued Speech Method

Cued Speech is a method used in conjunction with speech. The use of hand cues with accompanying speech is the hallmark of this approach (Paul and Jackson 1993). Eight handshapes are utilized in four positions on or near the face to supplement the spoken signal. It is a phonological model of English where the handshapes are associated with sounds (Goldberg 1995). The eight handshapes represent consonant sounds and the four positions represent vowel sounds. Individuals using this method combine these hand configurations and placements with natural speech movements to make the spoken language clearly visible to the cued speech recipient (Kipila and Williams-Scott 1990). By using the handshapes, one is able to distinguish between speech sounds that look similar when produced orally (Scheetz 1993). Because of its focus on speech production, some consider Cued Speech an oral approach (Gatty 1987).

Manual Method

Individuals promoting the manual communication method stress the use of gestures and sign language as the primary communication mode for deaf children. Children using this visual method use signs and fingerspelling to communicate their ideas. The signs used in this method could be American Sign Language or a sign system that is a manual code for English. The proponents of this method presume that the use of a manual means of communication such as sign language is effective in teaching language to deaf children. They believe that knowledge and understanding of language itself is more important than the ability to speak intelligibly (Mindel and Vernon 1987). The supporters of the manual method also believe that these children have a better chance of developing social and linguistic skills via sign language (Becker 1981). Approximately two-thirds of teachers of the deaf use some form of sign language in the classroom (Woodward and Allen, cited in Matthews and Reich 1993). However, very few deaf and hard of hearing children of hearing parents learn sign language from infancy when learning language is easiest and mastery greatest (Lane et al. 1996).

Types of Manual Methods

1. *American Sign Language (ASL)*: ASL is a manual, visual, gestural language with its own syntax and vocabulary (Jackendoff 1994). In fact, ASL is the fourth most used language in the United States (Christensen 1990). ASL's structure is different from English, making it a unique and independent language. In ASL, the visual capabilities of the eye and the motor capabilities of the body form the language (Paul and Jackson 1993). Manual signs represent concepts while nonmanual cues such as facial expressions, body movements, and use of the space in the environment are incorporated to express the meaning of the language. Its grammar relies on space, handshapes, and movement (Radetsky 1994). ASL is the preferred language for interaction among most individuals in the Deaf community in the U.S. (Newman 1992; Lane et al. 1996). Deaf cultural information is transmitted using ASL through conversations, storytelling, and videotapes (Padden 1980; Padden and Humphries

1988). Deaf adults who use ASL regard it as efficient, natural, and more aesthetically pleasing than manually encoded English signing systems, such as those used in simultaneous communication (Erting 1987).

2. *Simultaneous Communication (SimCom):* Individuals promoting the Simultaneous Communication (SimCom) method stress the simultaneous use of speech with manual signs to represent a spoken language. Proponents of this approach assume that it is possible to represent the spoken language visually. A person can choose from among a variety of manual sign systems to use simultaneously with spoken English: Signing Exact English (SEE II), Signed English (SE), and Pidgin Sign English (PSE) all can visually represent spoken English word order or portions of spoken English. Individuals supporting the use of SimCom believe that a deaf child can learn language in the same fashion as a hearing child—through the simultaneous use of spoken and visual forms of communication (Mindel and Vernon 1987). Proponents of this approach emphasize that providing both the oral and signing options simultaneously allows the child to learn language in a way best suited to his or her needs while developing communication skills to function in the hearing world (Mindel and Vernon 1987; Schlesinger and Meadow 1972).

   The disagreement over the best approach for educating deaf students with severe to profound hearing loss is not simply over which language is best to use, but rather, it represents profound differences in educational philosophy (Drasgow 1995).

3. *Total Communication Philosophy:* Total communication is a philosophy, a way of life (Cohen 1990). Total communication promotes the use of all possible communication methods (such as listening, speechreading, signing, using visual images, mime, etc.) to assist deaf children in acquiring language and understanding its use. "Total communication is a philosophy requiring the incorporation of appropriate aural, manual, and oral modes of communication in order to ensure effective communication with and among [deaf and hard of hearing] persons" (Conference of Executives of American Schools for the Deaf 1976, p. 358).

   Currently, English, either in spoken or signed form, is the predominant language in educational programs for deaf youth (Kannapell 1993). According to an investigation conducted

in 1992–1993 by Gallaudet's Center for Assessment and Demographic Studies, 56.1% of 48,300 deaf and hard of hearing children were receiving their education through speech and sign methods (SimCom) and 41.1% were being taught through auditory/oral approaches (Mahshie 1995).

4. *ASL/English Bilingual Philosophy:* In recent years, a debate has begun regarding the importance and value of bilingualism for deaf children. Supporters argue that a bicultural and bilingual approach will allow deaf children to use their natural sign language, ASL, as a means of learning English as a second language (Paul and Jackson 1993). In a bicultural environment, deaf children learn about famous deaf leaders and Deaf community customs and values. They also understand contributions made by deaf people, the historical aspects of Deaf culture, along with information concerning the majority, hearing world. The competent users of ASL, deaf adults, act as models for young deaf children (Drasgow 1993). Proponents of this approach believe that ASL is a symbolic badge of Deaf identity and that a knowledge of English is an important part of American life and culture (Higgins and Nash 1987).

In March 1994, the National Association of the Deaf (NAD) published a position paper supporting ASL and bilingual education. This paper proclaimed ASL to be the natural language of the American Deaf community. The authors emphasized that deaf children have the right to be educated, particularly with regard to reading and writing, in a bilingual or multicultural environment (Vernon and Daigle 1994). While the idea of using ASL as a first language and teaching English as a second language is gaining acceptance in theory, very little research has been done and very few programs applying this philosophy exist (Drasgow 1993). See chapter ten for further information on this topic.

Parents of deaf children need to consider all the approaches to communication. There is no clear evidence for the superiority of any of the various approaches for all or even most students with hearing loss (Paul and Jackson 1993). No one method is right for all children and their families (Goldberg 1995). Each family must choose the modes and approaches suited to its needs. Every child is different and each family system is different. Most important, the method chosen must be appropriate for your child's needs. For example, if your child has enough residual hearing that he or she could develop speech, you may decide to choose an oral approach. On the other hand, if your child does not benefit or benefits little from hearing aids, then you might decide to use a manual approach to communication (Boothroyd 1982).

Even though no one correct method exists for all children and their families, you must make a choice early in your child's life. The choice of communication method should not be delayed for too long after your child is diagnosed with a hearing loss. Consistent use of one method will enable your child to begin to acquire language and eventually become an active member of your family. Some professionals believe hearing aids should be used as soon as possible, regardless of the option chosen. If appropriate, once you have obtained the aids, you can continue to investigate your communication options (Ling 1984).

Take the time to explore your options thoroughly by gathering information from reading material, professionals (such as teachers, doctors, and counselors), other parents of deaf children, and most importantly, from deaf adults and adolescents. Gathering information from a variety of sources will help clarify your options and help you make an informed choice. You should also consider your family's attitudes toward deafness and the expectations for the child's role in the family unit (Kluwin and Gaustad 1992).

In all cases and in all choices made, you need to be motivated and willing to learn communication methods that are different from those to which you are accustomed. *The crucial issue is that hearing parents and deaf children don't automatically share a similar means of communicating* (Dolnick 1993). The mode you choose should give your child access to clear and understandable communication and actively involve him or her in the family unit.

Communication and Deaf Children

What is clear in research and practice is that deaf children process information visually. Hence, any approach to communication chosen by those significant to the lives of deaf children needs to include a visual means of transmitting information. Deaf children do not have access to auditory information and, therefore, they cannot naturally develop an auditory-vocal language such as spoken English (Erting 1987).

The visual component of communication is the key for deaf children (Bravin and Bravin 1992). Ways to enhance the visual aspects of language could include the use of space, movement, location, sign language, lipreading, visual images, eye contact, facial expressions, and body language. To illustrate this thought let us look at the idea of maintaining eye contact. Hearing people and deaf people use eye contact differently relative to what's acceptable in each culture. As an example, consider this story from a deaf friend who has a hearing daughter.

> During a conversation with her daughter, my friend naturally maintained a steady eye gaze. The daughter told her mother to stop looking at her. The daughter had to be taught that her mother needed to look in order to communicate. She apparently had not realized this and had been uncomfortable with her mother's need for staring (Meador 1994).

Contrary to this example, hearing parents may not maintain eye gaze with their deaf children because of a cultural belief about the inappropriateness of staring.

The visual aspects of language affect deaf individuals in another way. Deaf people need to shift their visual attention (their eyes) from the environment to the communication in order to receive a person's message. This shift in attention is called "divided attention" (Lederberg 1993).

> Suzie is eight years old and she is playing with her favorite game. Suzie's father wants to ask her about a part of the game that was missing two days before. Suzie must divide her attention between the game board and her father's communication so full understanding is obtained. Suzie's father knows that his daughter must look away at times while he is communicating with her so she can visually determine the main parts of her father's conversation.

It is important to remember that when playing with toys or interacting with others, deaf children must divide their attention between what is in the environment and the communication that is occurring. In contrast, hearing children can visually pay attention to the environment while simultaneously listening to someone speak (Lederberg 1993).

Divided attention has the following effects (Lederberg 1993):

1. It decreases the amount of interaction and communication between deaf children and their communication partners in a given time frame.

2. It causes hearing adults to be less responsive to a deaf child's attentional focus.

3. It increases the amount of time it takes to communicate when competing with the environment.

4. It increases frustration levels in hearing individuals who are not used to a visual means of communicating.

Divided attention is a natural phenomenon for all deaf people. This is how they visually attend to their world and learn. Hearing parents must be aware of this phenomenon and be sensitive to their child's needs.

Given considerations like divided attention, the way hearing parents communicate with their deaf children needs to change. Hearing parents tend to use an auditory-visual mode (relying on hearing and eyes) for exchanging information with their deaf children. This is the same mode used with their hearing children. Young hearing children with their hearing and their intelligence intact will be able to understand and produce their parent's spoken English language in a relatively short period of time (Axelsson 1994). Similarly, deaf parents tend to use a visual mode for communication. If the children's vision and intelligence are intact, then these children will acquire their parents' visual language naturally.

If children, whether hearing or nonhearing, have full access to their preferred mode of receiving information, they will acquire language. However, if a child does not have access to the auditory or visual channels by which the language is transmitted, the child will not acquire that language naturally (Mahshie 1995). Deaf parents of deaf children use a visual mode of communicating information. Deaf children need visual methods of communicating.

Deaf parents of deaf children are able to sustain communication in a visual manner by waiting until their child's visual attention is back with them before communicating again. This communication practice is not a natural habit for hearing parents because hearing individuals naturally use an aural-visual (hearing-vision) mode of communication. For example, some deaf children often communicate through gestures or signs when their hearing parents are not looking (Lederberg 1993). Visual communication may be missed unless parents become more alert to their visual surroundings. Additionally, deaf parents use physical touch in a unique way to get their child's visual attention. For instance, a deaf parent will place his or her hand on the child's body or tap the child's shoulder to gain visual attention before using speech and/or sign language. Hearing parents do not naturally use physical touch to gain their children's attention (Nowell and Marshak 1994).

The bottom line is that it is difficult to break old communication habits. Hearing parents of deaf children have faced this communication difficulty. They have described years of pain in not being able to communicate effectively with their children (Warren and Hasenstab 1986). Deaf children have as difficult a time grasping their hearing parents' spoken language as their parents have grasping their children's visual language needs. Communication is not a gift automatically given in infancy; it is acquired only by great amounts of labor and effort (Dolnick 1993).

Hearing parents of deaf children must learn new communication habits. In the Parent and Child section of this chapter, you will find guidelines to practice gaining and maintaining a child's visual attention during a communication interaction. Since deaf parents are naturally able to communicate with their deaf offspring, they are an important resource for deaf children and their families in providing access to Deaf culture and to language development (Henderson and Hendershott 1992).

When you are tense, tired, and/or frustrated, often it is easier to stop trying, to give up or say that it is not important. When this happens to you, it does not mean that you are insensitive to the needs of your child, but that exhaustion and frustration have taken a toll (Trychin 1990). Keep in mind that it is often hard to practice new habits, but the changes seen in your life and in the life of your child will make the efforts, labor, frustrations, and tired feelings worthwhile as you work toward family unity.

Today, the constellation of families is ever-changing. Some of these changes include divorce, more single parent households, and dual-career families. Not only are the family constellations changing, but also the amount of time we spend in family communication is dwindling. For instance, according to a report by a time management training firm in Pittsburgh, the average American husband and wife spend only four minutes a day conversing with each other, and the average working parent converses just 30 seconds a day with his or her children (Bodner-Johnson 1988). Now more than ever, due to family members being separated by space and/or time, there is a critical need for a family unit in which both deaf and hearing children can function. Each family has a structure which makes it unique. Each member must contribute his or her own uniqueness for the structure to become a family unit. As the number of families experiencing separation increases, so too does the importance of communication among family members. The increased level of separation among family members underscores the importance of "together time," especially dinnertime conversation. Deaf children may experience the feelings of separation and isolation even more acutely when they are not included in the family's everyday activities.

Children need stability within their lives. The family unit, no matter its makeup, provides for that stability. Stability is necessary for family unity to continue and thrive. All members of the family unit must believe that each person is an important part of family functioning and that each contributes to the stability of the family unit. Any change in the unit must be discussed openly and honestly with each of its members. Each change in the life of the family creates a time of challenge and an opportunity to grow. The family that faces the challenges together offers stability and unity to meet future challenges and changes. Family communication is at the heart of family stability and unity.

The following story is an example of how family unity works:

Jacob is a six-year-old deaf child. His three-year-old brother, Jason, and his parents are hearing. In their household, a weekly family meeting is held to talk about the decisions to be made concerning the needs of the family. For example, each family member gets to help plan the menu for dinner every week. During

this specific week, Jason chooses macaroni and cheese as his favorite dinner choice, and he and Jacob help to make this special dinner. Also, during this particular week, the family decides where they will go on their summer vacation. Jacob helps to map the course for their trip.

Jacob and Jason are active participants in family communication and therefore they contribute to family unity. Another way to increase family unity is to provide opportunities for your deaf child's siblings to experience your deaf child's world. Encourage them to try the following activities (adapted from Malcolm 1990).

1. Plan a visit to your deaf brother's or sister's classroom.

2. Take a tour of the audiology booth and receive a copy of an audiogram to take home.

3. Create a school display about deaf awareness or complete a school project on Deaf culture.

4. Start a sign language club at your school.

5. Upgrade the school library on deafness-related materials.

6. Suggest staging a school play with deaf and hearing cast members.

Additional Activities That Promote Family Communication and Family Unity

1. Make a family scrapbook or album that recognizes special events, school activities, vacations, birthdays, etc. Bring out the album once a month, discuss it, and add new information when possible.

2. Develop a family newsletter every few months or perhaps once a year. Your children can write articles for the newsletter and you can highlight their accomplishments. Over a period of time these newsletters can be mailed to extended family members or shared at family reunions.

3. Create family greeting cards that you can use for special celebrations or holidays. Each family member can contribute to the design.

(adapted from Medwid and Chapman Weston 1995)

7. Watch captioned television shows and movies with your deaf brother or sister and his or her friends. Invite your friends also and have a day at the movies!

Like a treasured painting where each color is essential to the image and each brush stroke provides a unique texture to develop visual harmony, so a family is celebrated by all members—each is essential to its stability, harmony, and unity.

PARENT AND CHILD

The importance of this chapter's contents in the lives of your child and your family can be summed up by the comments of a group of high school deaf students who responded to the question, "What is the most important, critical issue that you would tell parents about raising deaf and hard of hearing children?" Their response was a resounding, "Communication, Communication, Communication!" (Adams 1995). Listed below are guidelines for everyday communication with your deaf child.[1]

1. Eye contact is imperative when communicating with your child. Gain your child's visual attention.

2. Maintain your child's visual attention throughout the entire communication interaction.

3. Allow your child to orient visually at some point to the object of the discussion located in the environment. Then, wait until your child visually orients back to you before continuing the communication. Keep in mind the problem of *divided attention*.

4. Allow your child to lead the communication interaction; follow your child's communication leads (adapted from Jamieson 1994, p. 435).

These suggestions may seem like commonsense strategies to use when communicating with your deaf child. Believe it or not, most hearing parents resort to old patterns of communicating because

[1]These four guidelines are gleaned from the many available. Please use the references and resources listed in this book as well as deaf parents of deaf children and professionals in the field working with these children to determine other suggestions for effectively communicating with your children.

they forget to use the guidelines even after being taught them explicitly. Many communication breakdowns could be avoided if these simple guidelines were followed consistently.

POINTS TO REMEMBER

1. Dealing with feelings, understanding child development and behavior, and creating a family communication system are critical steps for a family whose goal is family unity.

2. In order for language to develop, you must actively seek out communication interactions with your child. These interactions can occur during such routines as getting ready for school, playtime, games, dinner, and bedtime.

3. Once a child is diagnosed as deaf, the family unit is no longer *hearing;* the family unit becomes *deaf and hearing.*

4. The single largest issue facing parents in maintaining a family unit is the task of involving all family members in communication in the home.

5. When communication is inadequate, the outlets for venting frustration and working through difficult situations as well as celebrating happy moments or subtle enjoyments are often limited.

6. Most children first experience and learn language through conversation and dialoguing with family members.

7. Some parents of deaf children have stated that they often feel as if they were teachers and not parents. A parent in the role of a teacher has limited time for dialoguing with his or her child.

8. Deaf children need information communicated to them visually. Because of this, hearing parents must develop new communication habits.

9. The choice of communication method used with your child is yours and yours alone. Your choice should be made after carefully considering what is best for your child and your family.

10. Some of your choices of communication methods include the oral/aural, cued speech, manual, ASL, simultaneous, and bilingual/bicultural approaches to communication.

11. Total communication is a philosophy that promotes the use of all possible communication methods (such as listening, speechreading, signing, using visual images, mime, etc.) to assist deaf children in acquiring and understanding language.

12. In all cases and all choices made, hearing parents of deaf children need to be motivated and willing to learn communication methods that are different than those to which they are accustomed. Hearing parents and deaf children don't automatically share a similar means of communicating.

13. Keep in mind that it is often hard to practice new communication habits, but the changes seen in your life and in the life of your child will make the efforts, labor, frustrations, and tired feelings worthwhile as you work toward family unity.

14. Family communication is at the heart of family stability and unity. The family that faces the challenges together offers the stability and unity needed to meet future challenges and changes.

15. A family is celebrated by all members; each member is essential to its stability, harmony, and unity.

■ Activities For Practice

1. a. An important activity that helps develop communication in the family is dinnertime conversation. This activity not only helps expose all family members to communication but it serves as a vehicle to include all members in family life. During your next meal time when all family members are present, set aside five to ten minutes for each member to share what is important to him or her. This sharing could involve a simple statement such as "I had a good day at school, today," to a more complex explanation of what was experienced.

    Describe below your experience with dinnertime conversation and how it affects your family:

    _____

    _____

    _____

    _____

———————————————————————

———————————————————————

———————————————————————

———————————————————————

b. Some families with deaf children have stated that they find it difficult getting all the children to attend to each communication. Some have chosen a signal device to help their deaf child and all other family members follow the conversation. Parents have used the communication spoon approach mentioned on page 55. And, some have used a simple hand gesture to point to the person who is communicating. It is critical to help your child visually attend to each communication.

List some things your family can do so that everyone can follow dinnertime conversation.

1. ————————————————————————

2. ————————————————————————

3. ————————————————————————

4. ————————————————————————

5. ————————————————————————

2. Another activity that helps families to communicate with each other as well as solve family conflicts is a weekly family meeting. During this meeting, all members can share information about what has happened in their lives as well as deal with troubling experiences and sometimes family conflicts. If you have not already done so, try to set up a time for a weekly family meeting. Even if you do not use this meeting time to resolve conflict, it could be a time set aside to discuss important family decisions such as a family vacation, a plan for the week, a time to discover what's happening in each other's lives, or just a time to be together.

3. One activity that is found to be fun for all family members involves developing a family scrapbook. Each week or once a month, each family member could bring something of importance representing what happened to them during that particular

time period. Before putting their items into the scrapbook, your children can explain why the items are important to them. This type of activity can help them practice good communication skills and can also show that each child is valued.

4. Another fun activity that deaf children have liked is using comic strips to enhance vocabulary and basic language skills. Your child will be more motivated to join in if the activities not only have a communication value but are also enjoyable at the same time. Take the Sunday comic section of your newspaper and cut out the comics that your child enjoys. Then cut out the word balloons for each picture. Mix up the pictures. Depending on your child's age, either have your child act out the scenes for the comic strip while putting them in the right order to tell the story or have your child write the words for each picture to create and tell the story. Another example is to make a video story with each family member picking a character to develop. You can list below other ways to create a story to involve your child in this kind of storytelling.

"Create a Story" Ideas

_____

_____

_____

_____

_____

_____

5. When a child must rely on vision to communicate, parents and child must adapt their communication styles. Parents need to adjust their communication behavior so that their children can see what they say and/or sign. Again, videotaping the interaction will provide you with feedback.

Using a 15-minute time period, try these behaviors when you interact with your child while he or she is involved in another activity and you want his or her attention. Then write down how you believe the interaction progressed as you paid more attention to your child's need for visual attention (adapted from Swisher 1992, p. 98).

a. Be facially animated and increase the size of your signs or gestures to attract your child's attention.

_____

_____

_____

_____

b. Allow your child sufficient time to look at other things in the environment when necessary.

_____

_____

_____

_____

c. Wait for your child's visual attention before signing and/or speaking again.

_____

_____

_____

_____

6. Storytelling is an excellent device to encourage interaction between you and your child. Whether you use a picture book, a fairy tale, or a family story you're passing on, telling stories to children is a unique experience that supports parent-child bonding, develops a children's vocabulary and language, stimulates their fantasy life, and develops critical thinking skills. Parents are encouraged to set a specific time during the day or evening to enjoy storytelling with their children. Many parents choose storytelling as a part of a nighttime ritual. You can get library cards for the entire family and have each child choose books that they have an interest in for the designated storytelling time. Also, remember that storytelling and acting out stories are an important aspect of Deaf culture.

7. As you practice some of the communication activities in this section or as you think about them, describe your reactions to the communication system in your home. What are the strengths in your system? What are the limitations to your system? It is important to evaluate your family's communication system on an ongoing basis so you can use some of the strengths to help family members to improve in areas that need work.

Strengths

_____

_____

_____

_____

Limitations

_____

_____

_____

_____

Chapter 6 | Your Child's Behavior— What Is Typical?

The previous chapter dealt primarily with family unity as it relates to early communication and interacting with your child. Now let us move on to a discussion of child behavior.

Growing up is a gradual process. Year by year your child develops in many areas socially, emotionally, cognitively, and physically. Your child's unique personality is heavily influenced by the learning that takes place each year. Yet this learning is but one factor that contributes to your child's personality and behavior. Other factors such as temperament, age, developmental rate, role, and position in the family also affect how your child behaves. Some youngsters are very active; others are very shy. Within the same family, children behave differently. Those of you who have several children can attest to this fact.

Parents are concerned about what constitutes "normal" behavior. The word *normal* is hard to define. Each child responds as no other to differing situations. Furthermore, what may be a normal response by a child to one situation may not be acceptable in another situation. However, certain behavior patterns do exist at different ages. In other words, particular ways of behaving generally characterize children at certain ages. These behavior patterns are the result of emotional, psychological, and physical changes that occur at those times.

This chapter presents the typical behavioral growth patterns for children between the ages of two and ten. These ages represent critical developmental periods in a child's life that will affect all future behavior and personality development. Growth and development does not begin at age two and end at ten. The process continues from conception to death. However, ages two to ten are extremely important years affecting the development of self and communication with others (Heimgartner 1982). Please note that the behaviors outlined are only guidelines. Each child is unique. Your child may progress differently from the patterns outlined.

Many life factors affect a child's behavior and personality. Physical characteristics with which a child is born, life experiences, and how parents have raised the child all influence behavior and personality development. A child's medical or learning problem also influences a child's behavior. For example, a child with a physical disability such as blindness or an educational disability that affects learning will have certain limitations placed on his or her world. These limitations have a direct impact on behavior. For instance, the blind child will be limited in tasks requiring vision (e.g., reading written materials, visually recognizing familiar locations or surroundings, etc.). A mentally handicapped child may find it difficult to make choices among many alternatives. Finally, an emotionally handicapped child may strike another child due to his or her inability to control anger.

Because limitations determined by a condition could influence a child's behaviors and activities, determining what behavior is "typical" is more difficult. When behavior is influenced by a condition, a parent must consider what is typical in light of the unique circumstances placed upon the child due to the specific condition.

First, it is important to review what behavior is more or less expected based on typical behavior found among children at the same age within the general population. This chapter will provide information to compare appropriate and inappropriate behavior at certain ages. A large portion of this chapter involves information about the different ages of a young child's life from the "terrible twos" to the relaxed tens. This chapter involves a large amount of information, much of which may be of interest to you. You should, however, focus primarily on your child's age range. If time permits, you may want to read the information presented for each level.

SKILL DEVELOPMENT

A child goes through many psychological, emotional, and physical changes. Behavior is often a reaction to these changes. As the body grows and matures, behavior grows and matures. Each year of maturity brings forth characteristics unique to that year. The calmness of age five-and-a-half and the creativity of age six give way to the inward characteristics of seven, the expansiveness of eight, and the self-motivation of nine. Finally, there is the reorientation period of ten (Heimgartner 1982).

A child who is deaf or hard of hearing displays the same characteristics as those of a hearing child. The point to remember, however, is that the behaviors mentioned at each age are general characteristics but will not apply to all children. Each child is an individual, and individual differences determine behavioral development. Many factors determine the way your child behaves, and hearing loss is one

of those factors. Always keep in mind the total child. A deaf child is a person first, with all the physical, emotional, and intellectual needs characteristic of hearing peers.

You cannot ignore, however, the effect that the hearing loss will have on your child's behavior. The experiences a deaf child has in English language development will also be reflected in his or her behavior in various ways. Specifically, the delayed English language development experienced by most deaf children can lead to more limited social interaction with hearing peers and possible isolation within the family unit if that unit only uses spoken English.

Social development and language are closely related. Delays in one area will most likely bring about delays in the other. Hearing children begin to understand how their behavior affects other people through verbal interaction. They are told by their hearing adult caregivers or peers that their behavior is appropriate or inappropriate. When deaf and hearing parents use a compatible means to communicate with their children, they also provide feedback about what is appropriate behavior. Deaf children in a hearing family where only spoken English is used and who have very little spoken language skills, must rely more on facial expressions and gestures in trying to understand another's reactions to them. Interpretations based on these nonverbal communications may be less accurate, and this may lead deaf children to give inappropriate responses. For example, a child who does not hear a person's tone of voice, which indicates a feeling or warns of possible wrongdoing, may not know that he or she is about to break a limit placed on behavior. Hence, deaf children with limited access to language interactions often have difficulty developing appropriate behaviors toward other people (Boothroyd 1982).

A deaf child displays the same characteristics that all children do. However, these characteristics must be examined in light of the effect hearing loss and his or her immediate environment has on behavior. Some researchers have noted their concerns regarding the social development of deaf children. These children have been seen to display behavior problems and social and emotional immaturity (Adams

1995; Bolton 1976; Boothroyd 1982; Broesterhuizen 1990; Liben 1978; Meadow 1980). Let us examine the possible reasons for this finding.

Family Communication

It is impossible to examine childhood behavior problems without understanding the influence of the family situation on the developing child (Frick 1993). One view about problem behaviors in deaf children is that these behaviors are a result of difficulties in family communication. As discussed previously, most parents (90%) of deaf children are hearing (Higgins and Nash 1987). The largest problem facing these parents is communication in the family. Problems in deaf children are seen as resulting from family communication breakdowns. Almost all family interactions, both healthy and not so healthy, are forms of communication (Murphy 1979). The behavior problems seen in these children may relate to frustrated attempts at communicating thoughts, feelings, and desires to their parents.

Some attempts at communication may be seen by hearing family members as inappropriate behavior. For example, suppose a five-year-old deaf child taps his grandfather hard whenever he wants his attention. The tap is not extremely forceful or harmful, but it is annoying. The grandfather believes the boy is being disrespectful and tells the boy that if it continues he will not take the child fishing. However, the boy is not being disrespectful. He is merely trying to communicate in a physical manner since he is not able to readily use spoken English to obtain his grandfather's attention (please see chapter eight to see how the grandfather, with knowledge about hearing loss and behavior management, handled this situation).

Hearing parents teach their hearing children how to behave by verbally communicating that information. Hearing parents who communicate fluently and clearly with their deaf children may still have problems communicating some important information about proper behavior because they primarily use spoken English in the home instead of sign language. When these parents communicate with people other than their deaf children, they often use spoken English. Deaf children may not be able to eavesdrop on their parents' conversations with each other or other people, so they do not have access to information about behavior and life attitudes discussed in this manner. It is likely that hearing children gain a broader understanding of their world by listening (eavesdropping) to the interactions between their parents and between their parents and other people in their environment (Lederberg 1993). Overall, hearing parents have been reported to use less communication and language in handling misbehavior and during social interactions with their deaf children (Connard and Kantor 1988). Research also indicates that low levels of positive parent-child interacting and involvement can be related to the development of serious behavior problems (Pettit, Bates, and Dodge 1993).

Etiology of Deafness

In the majority of cases of hearing loss, the etiology (cause) is unknown. Yet, the etiology of the hearing loss can cause problems in emotional and behavior functioning, as well as learning difficulties (Mcadow 1980; Vernon and Andrews 1990). Some of the known causes of prelingual deafness (meningitis, maternal rubella, and genetic syndromes) are also associated with other impairments, often neurological in nature (Heller, Flohr, and Zegans 1987). Neurological impairment can lead to behavior problems, learning disabilities, and emotional instability. For example, Attention Deficit Disorder (ADD), a condition that affects a child's ability to attend to a task, to control impulses, and to ignore distractions, has been linked to neurological impairment. When compared to hearing children, deaf and hard of hearing children have been found to have a higher prevalence rate of ADD.

Degree of Hearing Loss

Researchers view the degree of hearing loss as an important influence on a deaf child's behavior and development. Some investigators have found that a high degree of hearing loss (severe to profound) is associated with more behavior problems (Watson, Henggeler, and Whelan 1990). However, other researchers have found that children with lesser degrees of loss (mild to moderately severe) are rated by parents as having more behavior problems than those children with greater degrees of loss (Adams and Tidwell 1989). Hearing parents whose children have lesser degrees of loss may believe that their children can understand more of what is happening in their environment than they actually do because they use a hearing aid. However, these children may receive distorted information or they may misinterpret information. This situation may get worse over time due to additional frustration, and more behavioral problems may be seen. Parents of children with greater degrees of loss may understand that their children's hearing will not change. These parents may communicate with their children using a variety of means to make sure they are understood. Therefore, your expectations about what your child can hear or not hear along with the degree of your child's hearing loss can influence behavior and behavior management.

Behavior Problems and Parent Stress

Parents of deaf and hard of hearing children report having high stress levels. Additionally, child behavior often creates stress in the family. High levels of parental stress have been related to high levels of child misbehavior. A stressful environment may help increase children's problem behaviors as they react to their parents' stress. When a child's positive efforts to help deal with family stress are ineffective, the child may resort to negative behavior (Peeks 1992). Stress may also reduce most parents' tolerance of irritating behaviors (Adams 1995; Watson et al. 1990; Webster-Stratton 1993; Pettit, Bates, and Dodge 1993). Emotionally distressed parents may develop a negative mindset regarding their child's behavior and perceive that problems are worse than actually exist. Or, emotionally distressed parents may have difficulty in meeting their child's emotional needs (Watson et al. 1990).

The behavior problems of deaf children seen by parents, teachers, and many professionals are likely tied to the expectations these adults have for hearing children at the same age (Meadow 1980). The larger society in which deaf children function is comprised largely of hearing individuals, who establish rules for social interaction, define appropriate patterns for communication, and decide on acceptable behaviors (Scheetz 1993). It is extremely important for parents to view their child's development in relation to the influences that the cause of deafness, the degree of hearing loss, and the effectiveness of family communication have on behavior.

For instance, since an inability to hear affects a child's English language development, it means that the child may have difficulty communicating in spoken and written English. Difficulty in using spoken English will affect a child's behavior if this is the only method used to communicate in the family. Limited communication may result in seemingly inappropriate behavior from time to time. Children will often express their personal needs, relationship confusions, and desires about self and family through their behavior

(Androzzi 1996). A child will have more problems expressing his or her wants and needs. The child may be more physical in his or her reactions to the environment. Since a deaf child's communication is more visual than auditory or vocal, the child is more likely to use visual and physical ways to communicate feelings, ideas, and thoughts. While hearing children may yell and scream to get their thoughts and emotions across, deaf children may gesture, stomp their feet, or even hit along with vocalizing their ideas and feelings (Deyo and Gelzer 1987).

There are many possible reasons for the behavior problems seen in deaf children. Being aware of these causes may help you understand the problems better. And, understanding the causes of the behavior is a first step in doing something for you, your child, and your family.

Let's examine a typical situation that might occur between a deaf child and a hearing parent.

> The child wants to go outside because he sees a neighborhood friend playing in the yard next door. The child points excitedly to go outside. The parent says "No" because it is nearing dinnertime. The child, not understanding why it is inconvenient for him to go outside, begins to cry and opens the door to leave. The parent, not knowing the reason for the child's persistence in leaving, communicates "No!" once again. The child slams the door, screams and yells, and runs to the bedroom.

This behavior, seen by many as inappropriate, has developed from the communication misunderstanding between the parent and child. Frustration stemming from the child's inability to verbalize his wants and needs in spoken English and from the parent's inability to explain why the answer was no led to the child's physical and extreme behavior. This is only one example of how a hearing loss and limited family communication can influence a child's behavior.

An individual's behavior, and ultimately an individual's personality, is shaped by internal as well as external factors (e.g., physical characteristics, experiences, etc.). A child's ability to hear is as much a part of that child as are other characteristics such as eye color, height, body size, etc. The condition affects a child's behavior and personality just like any other aspect of his or her life. Additionally, the way in which parents and other family members view the child's

hearing loss will help determine the child's self-perception (Scheetz 1993).

Reviewing what is generally expected from children at each age will give you a basis for deciding if your child's behavior is appropriate or inappropriate. Taking into consideration your child's hearing loss, the cause of the hearing loss, your thoughts and feelings, your family's communication system and your child's immediate environment will help you understand the reasons for your child's behavior. It is still important, however, to decide which behaviors should continue and which should be stopped. Using information from what you know about typical behavior and your knowledge of hearing loss will help you make decisions about appropriate and inappropriate behaviors in your child.

Typical Behaviors

The following section describes the typical behaviors of children at particular ages. These descriptions will give you additional information from which to base your decisions on what is normal behavior for your child. Sit back, relax, and ready yourself for a journey focusing on the ways children, deaf and hearing alike, typically behave at specific age levels. Some events and information presented on this journey will be very familiar; others may predict events yet to come.

The Two-Year-Old

This is a "run-about" age. Motor skills are unevenly developed. Two-year-olds are constantly active and curious about the world and about their environment (Peterson 1982). Since children of this age are developing large muscle activity, they delight in rough-and-tumble play (Gesell, Ilg, and Bates-Ames 1977). The energy of twos seems endless. They do not sit still for very long and are unable to last at any activity for a long period of time.

Curiosity is the hallmark of two-year-olds. They touch and taste everything because this is how they learn about their world (Correspondence Course 1983). While two-year-olds gradually become more aware of the presence of others, they are unwilling to share their toys. A typical pattern is for them to cry and demand a toy, only to abandon it shortly for some new item or project. These children cannot place themselves in another's position. Statements like "just think how Linda feels now that you hit her," would have no meaning to them (Dixon and Stein 1992).

Because two-year-olds are so active, they require much supervision. If wanted toys or activities are not provided, two-year-olds will seek out and discover their own experiences. This may lead to a knocked over lamp or to the banging of utensils on pans. Typically, these youngsters tend to be hesitant, defiant, ritualistic, unreasonable, and impulsive (Gesell et al. 1977).

For your child, the use of gestures and/or manual communication may become an instrument of language because two-year-olds are able to express basic needs and wants (Heimgartner 1982). A rich gestural system will lay a foundation for developing language skills. Also, these children develop an ability to use their limited language creatively. They can pretend and begin to share ideas with those around them (Dixon and Stein 1992). However, the inability to communicate may lead to frustration, which is frequently released through temper tantrums (Brenner 1983). Deaf children from ages two through five have been found to display temper tantrums much more often than hearing children. These tantrums are often attributed to problems in early family communication (Gregory 1976).

The Three-Year-Old

Beginning with the third year of life, children become more conforming. Three-year-olds are less eager to take a room apart and are more interested in order (Correspondence Course 1983). They often enjoy putting things away in their proper places. They like to make choices. This is primarily due to the maturity of developing muscles. Three-year-olds have gained the physical ability to get around in their world. This period does not last for long, however. During the middle threes, the typical three-year-old may seem to turn into a different person. Refusing to obey is perhaps the most notable personality characteristic. The simplest and smallest of occasions can bring forth total rebellion (Gesell et al. 1977).

Imagination continues to develop at this age, and it will play an important role in playtime activities. This is an age when fantasy is important. It is not uncommon for three-year-olds to talk, play-out, or sign with imaginary friends or pets. Fantasy allows these children to "try out" new roles such as the opposite sex, parents, a monster, or an animal (Dixon and Stein 1992). Negative feelings can be expressed in safe ways. Storytelling is an excellent way to help your three-year-old to live out their fantasies that simultaneously enhance their language development. It also provides a time for family communication.

Three is a good social age for children. Children in the third year need other children such as relatives, neighbors, and friends from a play group (Dixon and Stein 1992). Three-year-olds want to please both adults and peers. Insecure, anxious, and, above all, determined and strong-willed, best describe the child who is rounding out the third year of life (Gesell et al. 1977; Heimgartner 1982).

The Four-Year-Old

The four-year-old may remind you of a more controlled two-year-old (Correspondence Course 1983). Four-year-olds usually do everything for a purpose. Motor activity is advancing and is evidenced through a great deal of running, jumping, skipping, and climbing (Gesell et al. 1977).

Four-year-olds are becoming more assertive with their world and on occasion they are bossy. Four-year-olds are also becoming more imaginative, and they often exaggerate. Telling tall tales, bragging, and tattling are common. Thinking often becomes magical. Fours often assign human feelings to objects around their environment (Dixon and Stein 1992). The four-year-old likes to be at center stage. Fours are very social and friends become important. Playing outside the home is extremely beneficial for both muscular development and showing off learned skills. Four-year-olds need to feel that they are important people. Praise and approval are needed at this age.

Four-year-olds also come to terms with their position in the family. Since these children are learning their role in the family, it is important to interact with them continuously. Letting four-year-olds share in structured routines and household activities is an important way for your child to understand his or her place in the family (Mindel and Vernon 1987).

Parental love is extremely important to four-year-olds. You will be tested, however, with extremes of behavior. It is not uncommon to see your child at one time saying, signing, or gesturing, "I hate you" and at another time saying, "I love you." Fits of laughter, and then rage are common. Fours like to observe adult reactions (Heimgartner 1982).

The Five-Year-Old

Fives are more friendly and more in control of their environment (Brenner 1983). Five is a self-contained age. Five-year-olds deal mainly with the here-and-now world even though it is complex. Five-year-olds are realistic and concrete. They are ready to begin formal schooling, being more eager to work than during the previous year. Parents may often describe their five-year-old as active, inquisitive, and creative. Their teachers may later describe them as restless, stubborn, resistant, and rebellious (Dixon and Stein 1992). Overall, their attention span has increased and they take pride in accomplishing tasks. Many times five-year-olds have high expectations and frequently will take on more than they can handle.

Five-year-olds are developing control over their world. Because they are curious, they constantly ask questions. Five-year-olds enjoy facts and information. Five-year-olds are ready to take on small responsibilities, and although they are helpful, they may become resis-

tant and sensitive if over-taxed (Brenner 1983; Gesell et al. 1977). A five-year-old also begins to show a sense of humor. A surprise joke on mom and dad is not uncommon. Five is also the age when children are happy and content with the familiar. Hence, these youngsters enjoy a set routine at home (Heimgartner 1982). Set routines help all children—deaf, hard of hearing, and hearing—to organize their world. These structured periods of the day set expectations in their minds that help bring order to their lives. For five-year-old deaf and hard of hearing children, structure and routine is vital in establishing order and expectations.

Five-year-olds also stay at a task according to interest level, (e.g., they may look at a picture book or work a puzzle for two minutes but play with friends for more than forty minutes).

The Six-Year-Old

Sixes are characterized by a high level of activity. They are at the threshold of exciting new intellectual and social experiences (Dixon and Stein 1992). Six-year-olds learn best through active participation (Peterson 1982). Six-year-olds are impulsive, active, excitable, and assertive (Gesell et al. 1977; Peterson 1982). Since activity is sometimes described as the hallmark of six-year-olds, they also tire easily.

During this year of life, there are many inconsistencies in conduct. Six-year-olds often behave in extremes, swinging from "love you" to "hate you" moods. Remember that six-year-olds experience changes in physical and psychological areas, for example, new teeth and changes in the body's nervous system. Six-year-olds are also vulnerable to a whole range of infectious diseases (Gesell et al. 1977). Thus, parents must know that some conflict is inevitable and normal.

Six-year-olds thrive on the security of routines established in daily life. In other words, they enjoy the familiar. These children often have difficulty making decisions (Gesell et al. 1977; Heimgartner 1982). They learn about the world mainly through imitation. Hence, they are highly dependent on directions and guidance from adults. Parents are encouraged to praise good behavior whenever possible. It would be wise to teach this child appropriate and inappropriate behavior through the use of stories about other six-year-olds rather than by a strong scolding (Gesell et al. 1977).

Six-year-olds abound with energy. They always seem to be running, jumping, and continually falling down. Sixes find it difficult to contain their energy and they often display impulsive and excitable behavior. This excess energy may at times cause deaf children to become frustrated when they experience communication difficulties. Six-year-olds often seem very noisy and loud. The loudness of the child's actions indicates the emotions stirring within (Heimgartner 1982).

This age is typically an excitable and noisy one for all children, but deaf six-year-olds tend to have even louder and noisier interactions with their environment. The lack of feedback concerning sound will tend to lessen their ability to "tone down" the noise they make. Remember that six-year-olds are learning to adjust to the demands of two environments—home and school. Within these environments there may be interactions with both hearing and deaf children, possibly for the first time on a consistent basis.

The Seven-Year-Old

Seven-year-olds develop slowly and steadily. Sevens are good listeners and are interested in others' feelings and attitudes. Seven-year-olds can be described as inward, self-absorbed listeners.

Personality development is important at this age. Sevens may appear to brood a lot and become withdrawn. They often complain about events or people. The need for independence begins to surface. Therefore, parents must supply the right balance of independence and support. Remember, these children are still very dependent on reminders and adult guidance.

Behavior problems are not usually prevalent at this age. However, mood changes from calm and good to angry and tearful frequently occur. Lying and stealing may occasionally occur (Brenner 1983). At seven, children start to develop a sense of ethics (Gesell et al. 1977). These new feelings and emotions are just beginning to take on meaning. They begin to understand that rules are a product of mutual consent (Dixon and Stein 1992).

Sevens are becoming more in control of themselves. Seven-year-olds never seem satisfied with their work. They appear to be perfectionists. This type of attitude carries on into their emotional development. Sevens are very sensitive, especially to the emotions and feelings of others. Seven-year-old deaf children are extremely sensitive to the expressions and body language of adults. Reading nonverbal language is important for these children in understanding the thoughts and feelings of others.

The Eight-Year-Old

Eight is an expansive age. Eight-year-olds show wide development in physical, social, and emotional areas (Gesell et al. 1977). Eight-year-olds are social and interested in others. These children are eager and enthusiastic. Activities involving explorations are common and eight-year-olds are very active indoors and outdoors. Eight-year-olds are evaluators of the events in their environment.

Since eight-year-olds are very social, activity with peers becomes important. Most conflicts of this age involve peer interactions. Arguments and squabbles with friends are common.

This is also an age when the ethical sense is developing and maturing. Eight-year-olds display simple feelings of shame, and their feelings are easily hurt (Gesell et al. 1977). Eight-year-olds, although far better self-controlled than younger children, still have difficulty grasping complex rules. Eight-year-olds are only beginning to draw conclusions and implications concerning the environment surrounding them. Some behavior problems seen at this age stem from the eights' impatience. Eights often display slight tempers. They also can be overly dramatic and they have a tendency to be argumentative. It is important for parents to be aware that eight-year-olds value a reward system (Gesell et al. 1977). Eights enjoy knowing when they have done well.

Eight is an age when children are outgoing. It is an age when children recognize their hearing loss and begin to accept it. They also begin to realize more fully the difference between themselves and hearing children (Scheetz 1993). Eight-year-old deaf children actively reach out to the hearing world for friendships (Heimgartner 1982). To effectively communicate to peers and adults is a vital goal for youngsters of this age.

Eights are also very dramatic. Thus, signs, gestures, and verbalizations are all exaggerated. There is an increased awareness of the ability to pantomime and of its benefits in play and communication (Heimgartner 1982). At the age of eight, drama and acting in plays are natural activities for deaf and hard of hearing youth. Engaging in role playing and putting on family plays are common happenings in homes with deaf family members.

The Nine-Year-Old

Nine-year-olds become more decisive, dependable, and fairly reasonable (Peterson 1982). Several important psychological changes take place during this age. Nines are developing self-motivation. Thus, they appear to have a reserve of energy to complete tasks again and again. Children of this age are not only able to continue on tasks for long periods of time, but they are also able to judge the job they have completed.

Along with certain changes in ability comes the development of new emotional patterns. For example, mood changes often occur. One day a nine-year-old is timid and cheerful; the next day this child is bold and grumpy (Gesell et al. 1977). In addition, the new emotional patterns often lead nine-year-olds to complain. Again, excessive complaining is most probably due to the growth process.

Nine is an age when strong feelings prevail. Nine-year-olds learn empathy, the ability to place themselves in another's shoes. Because of this new awareness and the development of other capabilities, nine-year-olds are better able to evaluate their decisions. It is not difficult to discipline nine-year-olds. Nine-year-olds can often be controlled merely by a look or by a short isolation period from other children (Gesell et al. 1977). Nine is a "settling down" age. Nine-year-olds exhibit control of emotions and of the environment. The child's personality is becoming apparent. Hearing loss, communication style, sense of humor, etc., will all be more noticeable as unique to the child's personality. At the same time, nine-year-olds are learning more and more about society. Nines are more aware of how individuals within society can behave toward one another. Nines are more aware of the prejudices of others (e.g., these children may get upset when excluded from games by hearing children). Nine-year-olds are impressionable, reasonable, and more independent (Heimgartner 1982).

The Ten-Year-Old

Ten-year-olds become more relaxed and content with themselves and with others. They are also more alert to both academic and social information.

The ten-year-old gives a fair indication of the person to be. Talents begin to surface and individual differences are readily apparent (Gesell et al. 1977). This is the age when the child's personality is significantly defined. Personality traits such as self-confidence are developing and becoming stronger. Parents are encouraged to reinforce the skills and talents of their ten-year-olds. Children of this age tend to have a strong sense of privacy. Secrets and private conversations with friends are common.

Ten-year-olds are entering preadolescence. Children in this phase are very different from children in the preschool and early school ages. The age range from nine to twelve is difficult to characterize because children all behave differently as they react to the physical and psychological changes they undergo during this time. Children of this age range can present their parents with a variety of problems stemming from disrespectful behavior, the need for approval from

peer groups, sense of humor, and for some, the beginning of puberty. Preadolescents display bursts of energy coupled with a release of strong emotions. Preadolescents can appear angry, giddy, foolish, and hilarious, but rarely are they calm.

Many parents refer to this age as the golden age. Ten-year-olds have a matter-of-fact attitude. Parents need to explain and clearly define firm standards since ten-year-olds still need consistency and consequences. Ten-year-olds are able to make connections between events and their consequences. However, if difficulties in family communication exist, parents need to make special efforts to clearly explain and communicate these connections in concrete, visual terms. Clear communication of ideas and information is needed most of all.

PARENT AND CHILD

This section contains some examples of typical statements that parents make about their deaf children's behavior. These statements reflect thoughts and feelings certain parents have regarding their child's actions. Following each statement is a discussion concerning the appropriateness of the child's behavior considering the child's age and hearing loss.

> *"All my child ever does is throw temper tantrums; this is not normal and it frustrates me."*—Mother of a two-year-old deaf child

A two-year-old hearing child also throws temper tantrums on a regular basis because of difficulty in communicating and understanding his or her needs. But deaf children tend to exhibit them more often not only because of lack of communication abilities, but also because of problems in family communication. It is important to note that tantrums can be expected of all two-year-olds.

"I don't understand what has come over my Joey. He used to be so active. Now he is very withdrawn and seems fearful of adults."—Parent of a six-year-old hard of hearing child

A child this age is usually eager to learn and explore the environment. Although we must remember that each child is different and behaves in a unique way, if there is drastic change in behavior, there may be a cause for concern.

"I do not know what is happening with Beth. She has been stealing money from her brothers and sisters. This must be because she is not getting enough of my attention. I will buy her more things."—Parent of a seven-year-old deaf child

This type of behavior from any child can have many different causes. It may be that the child is upset, or that (in this case) the child perceives that her sisters and brothers are the "winners" in the family. Thus, she feels the need to get back at them. Since this is the age when a child is maturing ethically, this behavior may also reflect the child's development in this area.

Remember that all behaviors have meaning and are communications from your child. Even if a behavior is a part of normal development, you need to teach your child about appropriate and inappropriate behavior. The behavior characteristics of each age are only indications of what may be expected from your child. Parent management of those behaviors is still needed to help guide the child in developing a sense of self-control.

POINTS TO REMEMBER

1. Your child's unique personality is heavily influenced by the learning that takes place each year. But learning is just one factor that contributes to your child's personality and behavior. Temperament, age, developmental rate, role, and position in the family also affect how your child behaves.

2. Certain behavior patterns do exist at different ages. These are the result of emotional, psychological, and physical changes that occur at particular ages of a child's life.

3. The behavior patterns presented at each age are only guidelines. Every child is unique. Your child may progress differently from the pattern.

4. A child goes through many psychological, emotional, and physical changes. Behavior is often a reaction to these changes. A deaf child will display the same characteristics as a hearing child.

5. Many factors determine the way your child behaves. Hearing loss is one of those factors. Family communication, causes of hearing loss, and parent stress are other factors influencing behavior.

6. A deaf child is a person first with all the physical, emotional, and intellectual needs of a hearing child. Do not let the hearing loss be the focus of your child's personality.

7. All behaviors have meaning and are forms of communication. But even if a behavior is characteristic of a certain age, it need not necessarily be tolerated. To develop a sense of self-control, children need to know what is appropriate and inappropriate behavior.

■ Activities For Practice

Do this activity one step at a time—a, b, and then, c.
1. a. During the next two days, take ten minutes toward the end of each day to write down the type of day your child has had. Specify behaviors you have noticed throughout the day.

Day One
(Date:)

_____

_____

_____

_____

_____

_____

Day Two
(Date:)

_____

_____

_____

_____

_____

_____

b. Check over the behaviors that you have listed in a., and mark
   down whether you consider these behaviors to be normal and
   age-appropriate or age-inappropriate for your child.

Behavior	Age-appropriate	Age-inappropriate
_____	_____	_____
_____	_____	_____
_____	_____	_____
_____	_____	_____
_____	_____	_____
_____	_____	_____

c. Compare the comments that you made about your child's behavior with the descriptions listed under your child's age in the
   Skill Development section earlier in this chapter. Are your
   views of your child's normal or age-appropriate behavior accurate? Are your views of your child's age-inappropriate behavior
   accurate? Write your comments here.

_____

_____

_____

_____

_____

_____

2. Look at the observations of your child's behavior you listed in the previous activity. Try to recall whether these behaviors have appeared in previous months or are new behaviors. Using this additional information, again decide on whether the behavior is age-appropriate or age-inappropriate for your child. Write your comments here.

_____

_____

_____

_____

_____

_____

3. Read the sample problem below. What do you think of this situation? Knowing what you know about the child's age and behavior, what do you think about this child's behavior?

A four-year-old hard of hearing child wants to buy a toy at the grocery store. The parent says, "No!" The child throws himself on the floor and screams and cries and will not leave the store unless carried.

_____

_____

_____

_____

_____

_____

7 Setting Limits

All human beings must learn restraint, in other words, how to limit their own behavior. Some things come naturally. Physically, children mature naturally. They progress from lying down to sitting, standing, and finally walking. This process of physical maturation requires very little help from parents (Brenner 1983). But other aspects of growing require direction and training from parents. As seen in chapter six, children behave differently throughout the growing process. Much of a child's behavior is learned (Kazdin 1984). Children need to learn the basic limits of their behavior. Depriving them of learning limits leaves them without the coping skills and possibly the opportunity to develop self-control. This leaves them helpless in a society that demands conformity to rules and regulations.

We often describe the process of setting limits on behavior as discipline. Appropriate behavior must be taught just like other behaviors. It is important for anyone who is involved with disciplining children to structure what children are to be taught. Your adult world was not designed with your child in mind. You are comfortable in the adult world because you know that much of what comes your way is more or less expected (Baker, Brightman, Heifetz, and Murphy 1976). Limits provide expectations for children and aid them in making their world a bit more manageable.

SKILL DEVELOPMENT

Children progress in their physical, emotional, and psychological capabilities through their lifetime. Children also progress with respect to their self-control learning what is appropriate and inappropriate behavior as they pass through certain ages. Although different behaviors are characteristic of particular ages, children still must know how to limit their behavior and develop a sense of self-control.

Learning self-control is much like developing any new skill. Uncontrolled behavior may be disappointing or even irritating to others in the environment. Children need guidance and limits in order to develop self-control so that they will be accepted in the world in which they live. Setting limits is necessary to provide for a child's safety and well-being. Limits also help the child to develop consideration for others (Correspondence Course 1983). Do not feel guilty about having to set limits on your child's behavior. When you set limits, you establish a secure atmosphere where learning can take place.

Most aspects of growing up require training. In this sense, a parent is a teacher. There is no magic formula for determining how to set limits. However, some structure or plan is necessary to teach your children what you want them to learn. To teach children about appropriate and inappropriate behaviors, you need to be very clear about limits. Common mistakes made in setting limits and managing behavior include using techniques inconsistently, rewarding undesired behavior, having unrealistic expectations for behavior, and modeling negative behaviors (Goldstein 1995). An important rule of thumb is that you must be consistent in applying rules or limits. For example, if you decide there are certain boundaries for outside play, be clear about why it is important to have such boundaries. And then be consistent about your decision.

You convey rules and limits about behavior to your children mostly through example and through clear communication (Ogden 1996). You also teach limits through developing routines. Most children like and prefer routines that structure their day. Hence, you need to structure mealtime, clean-up time, and bedtime so your child can develop and expect routines. This will bring order to your child's life. Remember that people act differently in different situations. People act differently at home, in school, at church, at a football game, in business meetings, driving a car, giving a speech, listening to music, or while eating dinner. Being specific about your limits is important because only then will your child know what your expectations are in a particular situation (Madsen and Madsen 1972).

Let us look at an example about setting limits. You decide that your child cannot watch television until after dinner. So in the late afternoon and during dinnertime in your home, between the hours of 3:30 p.m. to 6:00 p.m., the television remains off. Now, there can be several reasons for your decision. Perhaps this is a good time for your child to complete homework, to rest after a busy day, or to play outside to release energy. For whatever reason, you decide to set this limit.

When you set limits, it is important to state the imposed limits

in a positive form. It is natural for adults to use the word *no*. Your child expects to hear it. In fact, it is one of the first words a child speaks. *No* is a powerful word meaning "bad," "stop," or other negative things. When setting limits, however, this word is almost useless. To a younger child it commonly means the activity is bad. To an older child the *no* is interpreted as an order instead of a reasonable limit on behavior. The most important reason for avoiding the word *no* is that it tells the child what not to do, but does not say what the child may do. Therefore, it is advisable to state all limits in the positive. For example, instead of your limit being "No television watching from 3:30 p.m. to 6:00 p.m.," it may be "Television can be watched after 6:00 p.m. only."

Other examples follow:

Negative	Positive
1. No fighting with neighborhood children.	1. Only nice play with other children.
2. No swearing.	2. Use polite language.
3. No yelling and screaming in the house.	3. Talk quietly and softly or use a nice voice.

Stating your rules in a positive manner is the first step to providing clear limits on your child's behavior.

Rewards are important for letting your child know your rules have been followed and that he or she has acted appropriately. You can establish your own reward system using praise, hugs, extra playtime, etc., for maintaining the limits in your household (see appendix 2 for a survey to help you determine appropriate reinforcements for your child). In other words, whenever your children are doing what you wish, let them know it!

You may wonder what to do when your child breaks your rules.

Should you send your child to his or her room? Should you take away TV privileges? Do not wait until your child misbehaves to develop your limits. The more prepared you are beforehand, the easier it will be to help your child stop the misbehavior. Whenever possible, the action you take after the behavior (called consequences) should be logically related to the behavior (Canter and Canter 1985; Dinkmeyer and McKay 1989). You will more quickly teach your children appropriate behavior when the consequences you use logically relate to the misbehavior. When parents use logical consequences, they hold children accountable for their mistakes by helping them make up for their error in some way. Logical consequences teach children to be more responsible (Webster-Stratton and Herbert 1994). The following chart lists possible consequences for certain behaviors.

Misbehavior	Logical Consequence
1. Your seven-year-old willfully breaks your three-year-old's favorite toy.	1. Child must use his or her own allowance to buy another toy.
2. Your four-year-old uses a crayon to color the living room walls.	2. Child is required to clean the living room walls.
3. Your eleven-year-old steals an object from a store.	3. Child takes the item back to the store, apologizes to the store owner, then perhaps completes some chores in the store to help the store owner.

Each consequence must have a direct connection to the misbehavior. There are other points that you must remember when your child chooses to misbehave. First, whenever your child misbehaves, he or she should be given a choice to follow your limit. For example, "Scott, I cannot allow you to poke and hit your brother while playing. If you hit your brother again you will choose to sit and be in your room alone with no toys." You have now provided your child with a choice. If your child decides to continue to hit or poke, you simply say, "Scott, you hit your brother. You have chosen to go to your room." When you give your child choices, you provide him or her with the opportunity to learn the natural consequences of his or her behavior. Your child also learns to be responsible for his or her actions (Canter and Canter 1985).

In order to be consistent with your application of consequences, the consequences must follow every time the child chooses to misbehave. This is a critical rule to follow, but it can be difficult to do because children always test limits. Some children test them continuously, which is normal. A child needs to test limits in order to explore, discover, and learn (Correspondence Course 1983). This process helps your child to develop expectations about his or her world. Child management, frequently called *discipline*, is the means by which a child learns. Discipline is the procedure used to guide a child through safe and healthy channels (Correspondence Course 1983). You can begin to discipline your child by setting fair and consistent limits.

Listed below are guidelines (adapted from Webster-Stratton and Herbert 1994, p. 298) for using consequences:

1. Make consequences immediate.

2. Make consequences age-appropriate.

3. Make consequences nonpunitive. Setting logical consequences will help lessen the punitive nature of the consequences.

4. Involve your child in the consequence decision whenever possible.

5. Give the child a choice of consequences ahead of time.

6. Be sure you can live with the consequences you have chosen.

7. Quickly offer new opportunities for learning positive behaviors to be successful.

Discipline and Communication

All children need to learn restraint and control. Deaf children are no exception. Deaf children have the same needs as hearing children. They need to feel secure, loved, and important. The need for a healthy family environment, one which is physically and psychologically safe, is no different for a deaf child. All parents must explain the world to their offspring. However, parents of deaf children need to provide more explicit explanations (Mindel and Vernon 1987; Ogden 1996). This means that what you teach your child must be clearly demonstrated and communicated. Your child must clearly understand what is expected in specific situations. You must communicate limits to your child in a visual manner (drawings, gestures, signs, photographs, etc.) as well as use other ways to make explicit your explanations and expectations.

Your child has unique communication needs. Due to the hearing loss, you may be concerned about how to define expectations, limitations, and boundaries to your child. The relation of discipline to communication is a close one. Discipline itself is a communication process. This process relies on the language you use to convey your thoughts, feelings, and ideas. Early development of an effective language system will help you discipline your child. Many people view language as only involving the production of speech. But language involves both verbal and nonverbal (including visual) means of communication. A narrow definition of language is particularly confining when discussing language in connection with deaf children. Since your child's way of acquiring language is different from your own, it is important to capitalize on other channels of communication. The child uses channels such as vision, residual hearing, touch, distance, vocalizations, facial expressions, and body movements as avenues of communication (Proctor 1983). You can use these channels of communication to develop an effective language system with your child.

Developing effective language is related to the availability of life experiences. Language structures reality for your child and permits him or her to organize experiences in order to understand and control his or her environment (Boothroyd 1982). A child learns meaning first and then words. For example, a child can learn the meaning of *hot* when the child's hand touches hot water. The word *hot* is learned by connecting the word to the experience (i.e., the meaning). The important people in the child's life must help provide this meaning.

Everything a deaf child must learn, whether it be boundaries of playing outside or appropriate behaviors allowed before dinner, must be taught explicitly. Remember that most hearing children pick up acceptable behavior through imitation and from auditory cues. Children must be explicitly communicated with about appropriate behavior and shown how to act.

A deaf child must be taught proper behavior through the use of a visual means of communication (review chapters 4 and 5). It is important to know that since your child primarily uses a visual means to communicate, he or she will need full access to reading your body language, your facial expressions, etc. You will need to place some physical distance between you and your child so your child can visually attend to you. Often, hearing individuals get closer to each other when they are upset, frustrated, or intent in discussion. Your child

needs to be able to read you visually by attending to your eyes, lip movements, and body language to receive the full meaning of your message. Also, your child must be shown meaning through photographs, drawings, demonstrations, and modeling to develop an understanding of the world's boundaries. For example, you can show your child what appropriate behavior is expected by demonstrating proper behavior in the play area (e.g., handling toys gently, using crayons only with paper), and you can also illustrate proper behavior or limits on behavior by drawing pictures. You can make this a fun activity for your child and include them in on the limit-setting experience by having him or her draw the pictures.

You can also use a camera and take pictures of your child acting out appropriate and inappropriate behaviors. These pictures can be used as a base for teaching behaviors you want to continue and preventing behaviors you don't want to occur. The photographs can also be used with the list of rules to define what behaviors are allowed and which are not. These snapshots will explicitly convey to your child the expectations you have for behavior.

Communicating limits to any child is not easy. But parents who are successful give clear guidelines and limits to their children through discussion and explanation. And these parents believe the extra effort is worthwhile. Keep in mind that children will test even learned limits. A child with expressive oral language will verbally test the limits while a child without expressive oral language will test more concretely (through physical contact, a spilled dish, etc.) and may give the impression of being less well behaved (Boothroyd 1982). A deaf child needs to test limits in order to discover and understand the world and give meaning to it. Teaching your child limits can be difficult. You must provide more explanations for your child by example, drawings, gestures, signing, or whatever visual and oral methods you believe are effective. This probably means that your task is to develop a better sense of your child's environment by being more attentive to it.

PARENT AND CHILD

The following situations illustrate limit setting by parents of deaf children. Review the parents' use of rules, explanations, and consequences when setting limits for their children. Remember that each rule should be stated in the positive and the consequences should be logically related to the behavior.

Behavior	Limit	Explaining the Limit	Consequences of Breaking the Limit
A nine-year-old loves to paint pictures. The child enjoys painting in the family room with members of the family present.	Use proper care while painting (specifically, lay down papers, keep paint brushes in container, etc.).	Parent draws a picture of a neat painting area—brushes are shown in a container, all sheets of trash are placed in a trash can, etc. He also draws a picture of his child, smiling, within the area.	Child will paint in the basement during the next play session, or child will not be allowed to use the paints during the next play session.
A twelve-year-old boy wishes to stay awake an extra hour (until 10:00 p.m.) on weekend evenings.	Child must be in bed by 10:10 p.m.	Parents demonstrate through examples that the child must be in bed by 10:10 each evening. Using a portable clock with a large face, the parents point to the clock at 10:00 p.m. Child is then shown that he must wash, brush his teeth, change his clothes, and be in bed by 10:10 p.m. The parents point to the clock again showing the time limit.	Minutes will be deducted from the next evening's time limit. For example, if the child is five minutes late (gets in bed at 10:15 p.m.), he goes to bed five minutes earlier the next evening (must be in bed by 10:05 p.m.).

Behavior	Limit	Explaining the Limit	Consequences of Breaking the Limit
A four-year-old girl wishes to play with a friend in the backyard. However, she has difficulty sharing. She gets angry when other children want to play with her toys.	Nice play only in the backyard.	Mother and father model good sharing and playing behavior for the child. The child is shown how two people can enjoy playing together. Also, the child is shown proper ways to play with toys and ways to share with other children. The four-year-old is also praised with words, smiles, and hugs when sharing and playing appropriately.	Child is removed from playtime when she refuses to share. Child will play alone the next time she plays in the backyard. She is not allowed to play with the toys she would not share for a designated time period. Child is kept inside during the next playtime.

POINTS TO REMEMBER

1. Physically, children mature naturally—they progress from lying down to sitting, standing, and then to walking. This process occurs with little help from parents. However, other aspects of growing require direction and training from parents. Children need to learn the limits of their behavior.

2. We often describe the process of setting limits on behavior as discipline. Appropriate behavior, like other behaviors, must be taught.

3. You must set limits to provide for a child's safety and well-being and to help your child develop consideration for others. Do not feel guilty about having to set limits on your child's behavior.

4. You must develop a structure or plan to teach your child what you want him or her to learn. To teach your child about appropriate behavior, you must be very clear about limitations.

5. People act differently in different situations. We act differently at church, in school, when listening to music, in business meetings, while eating dinner, etc. Being specific about your limits in different situations is important.

You must be consistent in applying rules or limits.

7. A child will test limits in order to learn or discover about his or her world.

8. All children need to learn restraint and control. Deaf children are no exception.

9. Parents of all children must explain the world to their offspring. Parents of deaf children, however, need to provide more explicit, visual explanations.

10. A deaf child needs to test limits in order to discover and understand the world and give meaning to it. Teaching your child limits is not easy.

■ Activities For Practice

1. We act differently in different settings. List three specific situations your child is continually involved in. Examples include sitting at the dinner table or playing in the play area. Now decide on two limits that you would place on your child's behavior and list these for each specific situation noted. Be sure to state limits in a positive way.

Example:

Situation
Sitting at the dinner table

Limits
1. Being seated is necessary at all times.
2. Use polite table manners.

Situation

A. _____

Limits

1. _____

_____

_____ 2. _____

_____ _____

B. _____ 1. _____

_____ _____

_____ 2. _____

_____ _____

C. _____ 1. _____

_____ _____

_____ 2. _____

_____ _____

2. Using the information you provided for activity 1, decide how you can best explain these limits to your child. In what ways would you clearly convey these rules to your child? Develop these thoughts further by explaining details about how you would or already do convey the limits you set.

_____

_____

_____

_____

_____

_____

_____

_____

_____

3. Review the six limits you have listed in the above activities. Are these limits important in the long run? If they are, take three of the limits listed and decide on the consequence you would place on the child if each limit is broken. Try to connect the consequence logically to the misbehavior.

Example:

Limit	Consequences of Breaking Limit
Only careful play with toys permitted.	Child cannot play with toys for one day. OR Child must replace toy with his or her own money.

Limit	Consequences of Breaking Limit
1. _____ _____	_____ _____
2. _____ _____	_____ _____
3. _____ _____	_____ _____

4. Read the sample problem below. Given what you know about limit setting, what steps would you take to limit your daughter's behavior? How would you handle this situation?

    Your ten-year-old deaf daughter has difficulty doing her chores around the house. She does her work sometimes and other times does not. She tells you she is tired, or that she wants to meet her friends, or that she must do her schoolwork.

_____

_____

_____

_____

_____

_____

_____

Understanding Problem Behavior: Knowing Your ABCs

All parents are concerned about their children's behavior. Parents who establish clear limits and consistently enforce those limits with clear communication take the first step in structuring their offspring's world so that learning can take place. Chapter seven discussed the importance of setting limits and how to follow through when children test these limits. General guidelines and basic principles were given for limit setting (the fundamental groundwork for the day-to-day practice of discipline). Sometimes, you will need to go beyond basic limit setting to determine how to stop or prevent problem behaviors from occurring and to set up an environment for positive behaviors to result. This chapter will help you examine problem behaviors and help you decide on how to best stop behaviors or prevent them from happening and to replace them with appropriate behaviors.

SKILL DEVELOPMENT

All parents are in the business of changing, modifying, or limiting their children's behavior. What determines success is whether you use a plan to change behavior. Systematic use of a plan will give purpose and direction to methods you have probably used for a long time. If you consistently follow your plan, you will achieve the desired results. For example, consistently having your child follow the rules and limits in your house will provide expectations for his or her world and establish a base for success in managing behavior. The most difficult part is consistency. But following a plan helps make what you do clear to you and your child. And a plan aids in making your actions consistent. The A-B-C framework is such a plan.

The A-B-C Plan

Before changing a child's behavior, you must first carefully observe that behavior to understand it and see more clearly what needs to be changed. In order to change behavior, you will need three pieces of information (Baker et al. 1976):

1. The setting in which the behavior takes place (antecedents);

2. The specific behavior that occurs (behavior);

3. The actions that follow in that particular setting (consequences).

If you know the setting in which the behavior occurs, the behavior, and the actions that follow the behavior, you will more clearly understand if the behavior will continue.

Antecedents

You must view the behavior you want to change within the context (setting) in which it occurs. You should also know what triggers a given behavior. You will then know the behavior's antecedents. The same behavior occurring in different contexts is handled differently. For example, you handle a child crying when there are no lights on in a dark room differently from a child crying because of a barking dog.

Behavior

Behavior is what you first see when observing your child. Behavior management assumes that observable behaviors are good targets for change (Goldstein 1995). First, you must decide whether your child is displaying a "problem behavior." If you decide he or she is, it is time to observe the behavior in detail. To change a behavior, you must know what you want to change. You need to clearly identify the behavior that you see. As an agent of behavior change, you must learn to specify, in exact terms, the problem behavior (Baker et al. 1976; Kazdin 1984). For example, a mother might complain that her eight-year-old is fussy before dinner every evening. "Fussy" is a general term that means different things to different people. Further discussion might reveal that the mother actually means that the child cries when asked to come to dinner. "Cries before he comes to the dinner table" is a specific behavior that others can easily observe. Specifying the behavior is the first step to developing a plan for behavior change. Descriptions like "acting aggressive," "stubborn," or "fussy," are not specific; they do not pinpoint the child's problem behavior.

When trying to understand behavior, remember that no two children are alike; each child is unique. Behavior is the way your child tells you what he or she needs or desires. Hearing loss limits the opportunities for expressing those needs using oral language. Hearing loss does not make your child different; it adds to your child's uniqueness.

You need a consistent framework to change your child's behavior. You can obtain consistency by keeping your child's daily routines as stable as possible. Let your child know his or her part in the overall plan of management within the home. Structure in your home will help your child develop expectations about the world. Setting limits will also help your child develop these expectations.

Consequences

Consequences are the actions that follow a behavior. Behavior is maintained, changed, or shaped by the consequences of that behavior (Goldstein 1995). Quite often the consequences determine whether a behavior will happen again and how often. For example, behavior that is followed by something pleasant (a positive consequence) is likely to happen again (Baker et al. 1976; Herbert 1981). Consequences include actions such as approval (rewards), disapproval (punishment), ignoring, or threats. Some rewards are praise, money, activities for enjoyment, and candy. Some punishments are taking something away that a child likes, scolding, and removing a child from a fun experience.

There are no universal rewards or punishments. Every child is different. Your job is to discover the most effective rewards and punishments for your child. How effective a given consequence is in a situation with a given behavior can be determined only by each child's experience. In other words, through your interactions with your child, you will discover which consequences work and which do not.

The foundation of behavior management is consistency. The A-B-C pattern is a framework that provides guidelines for consistency. Read the examples of the A-B-C pattern in the chart on page 108 and examine each part of the pattern to determine how this system works. Can you predict what will happen in the future for each case? Use the principles of behavior modification to make your prediction. Remember, behavior that is followed by a pleasant outcome is likely to happen again. Behavior that is not followed by something pleasant or rewarding will be avoided.

Looking at the chart, you can predict that Joey's behavior is likely to happen again because Joey received a positive outcome (attention) from his behavior (crying). Sally's demonstration of affection to her

A Antecedents	B Behavior	C Consequences
Mom and Dad are pre-paring dinner and are talking. Joey gets no attention.	Joey cries before dinner.	Mom and Dad stop what they are doing and go see what is wrong. Joey gets attention.
Grandma arrives for a visit.	Sally runs up and gives Grandma a kiss.	Grandma gives Sally a dollar bill.
Dad asks Julie to do the dishes before she goes out with her friend.	Julie goes out without doing the dishes.	Julie is grounded and is not allowed to go out with her friend for one week.
Tommy was to share his new bike with his brother at certain times.	Tommy was reluctant to share, but did so anyway.	His brother never dis-played appreciation; his parents made no com-ment and did not notice.

grandmother will also likely happen again because of her grandmother's rewarding response. On the other hand, Julie's disobedience may stop because of the negative consequence of her actions. And, finally, Tommy is likely not to follow through on his bargain in the future since his behavior went unnoticed.

Using the A-B-C Plan

The A-B-C pattern can provide a consistent framework to help you apply limits. Again, remember that your child will repeat any behavior that brings good outcomes. Deaf children have the same needs as hearing children. In applying a set of rules to deaf children, you must remember that communicating ideas and getting your points across will take extra time. This is the reality of hearing loss. Ideas and issues taken for granted in raising a hearing child through use of an auditory-visual mode of communication must be made explicit using visual means for a deaf child (Mindel and Vernon 1987; Ogden 1996).

The A-B-C pattern offers a framework for establishing consistency and for making explicit the rules necessary to change your child's behavior. Hearing loss has little negative effect on the success of behavior-management techniques such as the A-B-C pattern (Algozzine, Schmidt, and Mercer 1981; Belcastro 1979; Mira 1972).

However, you do need to be more careful in pinpointing which behaviors are problems and which are not. Sometimes what may appear to be a behavior problem is in reality an attempt to communicate. For example, your child may continually tap or hit you while speaking to you in order to gain your attention. You can correct this behavior by looking at your child when he or she is talking. Otherwise, your child may fear that you have missed something. Careful observation of the behavior (specifying exact behavior) within the setting in which the behavior occurs (antecedents) and noting what happens after the behavior occurs (consequences) can help you pinpoint the severity of the behavior problem and what helps it continue.

The A-B-C pattern is mainly used to develop consistency so a behavior problem can be changed. This pattern is particularly effective with deaf children because it does not rely on the spoken English language for its success (Mira 1972). The following example illustrates how a mother of a deaf seven-year-old can use the A-B-C pattern to identify a problem behavior.

A Antecedents	B Behavior	C Consequences
The child grabs an item (food, toy, etc.). The mother pulls it away. She says, "No!"	The child cries, whines, and stamps her foot. A temper tantrum occurs.	The mother gives the item to her child to stop the problem behavior.

This child's behavior is highly inappropriate for a seven-year-old. Identifying the behavior is part of the modification process. Using the A-B-C pattern, the parent can examine the setting in which the temper tantrum occurs and what happens following it. After identifying the antecedents and/or consequences that help the behavior continue, this mother can determine how best to alter the pattern to stop or decrease the misbehavior and create the desired behavior.

Parents must become detectives as they interact with their children. Problem behaviors are nothing more than the successful ways your child has learned to get what he or she wants from the environment (Baker et al. 1976). In order to do your detective work thoroughly and completely, you must examine the behavior pattern from your child's point of view. To you, behaviors such as screaming at and chasing your child are not pleasant consequences. To your child these consequences may be positive reinforcers because they cause you to give your child attention. As we know, behaviors that are followed by positive reinforcers are more likely to happen again. Reviewing and investigating the causes of behavior in deaf children is done in the same manner as with hearing children. However, as mentioned earlier, there are a few considerations that you might want to keep in mind when dealing with deaf children.

Techniques for Altering the A-B-C Plan

Antecedents You can often prevent or stop a misbehavior by changing the setting (the antecedents). Let's look at some examples.

A father knows his child and a neighbor child both like the same toy (the antecedent). He removes the toy from the play area before the children enter.

A mother is aware that her child usually is very tired after school. During this time, the child is easily frustrated, irritated, and extremely argumentative. The mother directs the child to take a nap (the antecedent) before continuing the day.

The mother of a five-year-old child is distraught because of her son's temper tantrums. The mother observes that each time she asks her son to do something when he is involved in an activity, he does not respond. As the mother continues to talk, her voice grows louder and louder as her son ignores her requests. When the mother finally reaches her limit, she puts away the play material. The little boy then has a tantrum.

After a careful review of the situation, it becomes obvious to the mother that the play items (the antecedent) distract the boy from responding. The mother decides to rearrange the setting by removing all distracting items such as toys, television, and books when she wants to teach her son how to respond appropriately. She then rewards her son whenever he responds in the appropriate manner.

In the last example, the mother rearranged the environment or setting to prevent the behavior from happening. It is also important that we promote appropriate behaviors. For example, we not only want to stop the five-year-old from having a temper tantrum, but we also want to reinforce (reward) him for responding appropriately to his mother. The survey in appendix 2 will help you find possible reinforcers to use with your child. Add to the list as you find specific

consequences that are good at reinforcing your child's appropriate behavior.

In many instances, when antecedents are changed, the misbehaviors decrease. To illustrate this point, let's take the example of a father of a seven-year-old deaf boy.

The family moves into a new home. Since the move, the boy cries and appears frightened when it is time for bed. This behavior occurs at least four times per week. The boy's father decides he and his son will look at a storybook at bedtime in order to tire the boy. To the father's surprise, the crying episodes increase rather than decrease.

An examination of the settings in which the behavior occurs reveals that the crying never happened at the old house. In the previous home, the boy's room was positioned in the opposite direction from his new room. It faced the street and was dimly lit by streetlights. The new room faces the backyard and has no source of light. This room is very dark when the lights are off. In the dark silence, the deaf boy is not aware that his parents are nearby. Hence, he cries when he does not immediately fall asleep. The boy's father thinks his presence is needed to give the boy security. However, the attention received from the father increases rather than decreases the behavior. Placing a night light outside the boy's room enables him to fall asleep and decreases the crying episodes.

You must carefully examine the impact of the hearing loss on the antecedents of behavior. Try to discover how a hearing loss influences the situation or the antecedent events. Only then can you properly alter the events in your child's life to change the behavior. In the example shown above, the child's hearing loss blocked out all auditory information. Therefore, when the lights were out, the boy experienced a sense of being totally alone. The light from the night light assured the boy that his parents were nearby.

Behavior Some behaviors are common to deaf children due to cultural and language differences. You must become aware of these types of behaviors and the reasons for their occurrence.

> A four-year-old deaf child makes several shrill noises when she is unable to watch television. The mother usually gives her more time to watch television in order to stop her daughter's shrieking. The shrieking continues and even increases during times other than when the child wants to watch television. She displays the shrieking behavior while playing, when eating, etc. The mother decides she needs a plan to decrease this annoying behavior. Her plan involves the use of time out (removal of the child from the situation so no reinforcement can occur). She uses this technique consistently. She also attempts to reinforce appropriate behavior when the shrieking behavior does not occur. The mother demonstrates to the daughter the proper ways to watch television, have a snack, or play during the times that are appropriate for such activities. The mother also makes a picture board for each day's scheduled events. When the child appropriately points to the picture when it is time for the activity, she is rewarded. The girl is also rewarded (by points or stars) for appropriate behavior during the specific activity. With these extra points (stars), she is able to buy more time to do the activity during that day or later.

The shrieking behavior displayed by the girl in the above example results from the breakdown in communication between her and her mother. Her mother determines that this behavior is annoying and in need of elimination. Some problem behaviors exhibited by deaf children may result from their inability to express themselves when family communication breaks down. It may be necessary to target these behaviors for change and to replace them by practicing with the child more appropriate methods for communicating wants and needs.

There are several instances where deaf children's behaviors are labeled as inappropriate or odd when, in fact, the behavior is common to most individuals who are deaf. For example, a child's inability to hear and monitor his or her speech may lead to speech that is too loud or too soft. Or the child may make strange vocal sounds, clicking noises, grunts, or hums without being aware of it (Higgins and Nash 1987). Often parents have complained that eating habits and related sounds made are especially difficult for their children to monitor. All of your child's behaviors must be examined in relation to the hearing loss, communication, and your child's cultural experiences. For instance, since deaf children will have difficulty monitoring their voice levels, hearing parents will need to help them monitor their voice levels in various social situations (e.g., when dining out in a restaurant).

Consequences It is important to place specific, logical, and consistent consequences on your child's behavior to help your child know what to expect when he or she behaves in a particular way (review chapter seven about logical consequences).

Consequences, for the most part, involve the use of rewards (pleasant outcomes) and punishments (unpleasant outcomes). Once you've identified the consequence for a specific behavior, focus on how to remove the pleasant outcomes that reinforce that inappropriate behavior. The three most frequently used unpleasant consequences to decrease problem behavior are (1) ignoring the behavior, (2) punishing the behavior, and (3) giving time out.

A pleasant consequence, or positive reinforcement, should always be used to replace unwanted behavior with wanted behavior and to develop positive behaviors in your child. Therefore, positive reinforcement will be discussed prior to unpleasant consequences.

Using Positive Reinforcement

We will start with the concept of positive reinforcement because behavior that receives a pleasant outcome is likely to happen again. Positive reinforcement will help strengthen behavior. It can be used to increase good behavior that a child displays or to help replace an inappropriate behavior with a more appropriate one. It is easier to increase behaviors than to decrease them (Morgan and Jensen, cited in Goldstein 1995). Therefore, always use positive reinforcers such as praise, hugs, smiles, stickers, favorite activities, and other rewarding experiences to help increase your child's appropriate behavior. The following guidelines (adapted from Rhode, Jenson, and Reavis 1992; Webster-Stratton and Herbert 1994, pp. 249–250) will help you remember to use positive reinforcers.

1. Reinforce your child immediately for his or her good behavior. The longer you wait, the less effective this consequence will be. Don't forget to praise when your child is playing or working quietly.

2. Reinforce your child frequently. It is especially important to do this when your child is learning a new skill. The reinforcement could be as simple as saying, "Good job!"

3. Use enthusiasm in giving the reinforcer. Enthusiasm indicates to your child that the reinforcement is important. Praise with smiles, pats, hugs, and kisses as well as signs, gestures, or spoken words.

4. Give praise without sarcasm and qualifiers.

5. Maintain eye contact. It suggests that your child is special and has your total attention. Eye contact in itself is often reinforcing, indicating you care and that you are interested.

6. Describe the behavior that you are reinforcing. It is critical that the appropriate behavior is clearly understood by your child. Being explicit tells him or her what is consistently expected.

7. Build anticipation and excitement about receiving a reinforcer. It helps motivate your child to behave appropriately.

8. Give positive reinforcement in front of other people. Don't be concerned about spoiling your child with too much praise.

9. Vary the reinforcement. Just like adults, children get tired of the same things. It is necessary to change the reinforcers at times to keep them effective. Letting your child choose which reinforcers he or she likes helps make the variety of reinforcers more potent for success.

10. Model positive reinforcement for your child by recognizing your own achievements.

Using Unpleasant Consequences

Ignoring Unwanted Behavior Ignoring a behavior removes the attention that serves to reward your child for misbehaving. For example, if your child cries when put to bed, the crying will gradually decrease and eventually stop if the behavior (the crying) is ignored. If a brother continuously teases his sister and she learns to ignore her brother's comments, the teasing will gradually decrease and eventually stop. Thus, ignoring the behavior tells the child that no reward or reinforcement will follow the misbehavior. Certain behaviors, however, cannot be ignored because they are harmful to the child or others. For example, it would be unwise to ignore a child who hits himself or herself or others. Alternatives to ignoring would be in order.

The following guidelines (adapted from Forehand and McMahon 1981) will help you ignore unwanted behaviors.

1. *Refrain from making eye contact or giving nonverbal cues.* When a child is involved in a behavior that you would like to change, it is often difficult to ignore the activity. Your child may anger you or even appear rather cute. Whatever the reason, you may inadvertently reinforce this inappropriate behavior with a brief smile, a frown, or even a glance at your child. Taking away eye contact prevents you from communicating with your child. When you ignore a behavior, turn at least 90 degrees and preferably 180 degrees from your child so no eye contact can be made.

2. *Do not make communication contact.* You should not make any contact with your child while he or she is involved in an inappropriate behavior. Often your child may ask you why you are ignoring him or her. You can offer an explanation at a later time. Communication contact only offers the possibility of reinforcing the unwanted behavior.

3. *Do not allow physical contact.* Your child will often try to initiate physical contact once you have started to ignore him or her. Your child may tug on you, attempt to sit on your lap, or try to touch you when you are ignoring. It is a good idea for you to stand when you are ignoring a behavior. Your child won't be able to sit on your lap and this may indicate to your child that you are definitely ignoring him or her rather than being involved in another activity.

Punishing Inappropriate Behavior Punishment removes a reward (reinforcement) or places a negative consequence on behavior. Removing a reward from a child is an effective way to reduce the occurrence of problem behaviors. This technique is most effective when, after removing a reward, you give your child a way to earn back the reinforcer (Baker et al. 1976; Canter and Canter 1985). This way your child does not fear or avoid you when you are punishing him or her.

Also, your child is encouraged to practice the appropriate behavior in order to regain the reward. You should also warn your child to stop the misbehavior before you punish it. Consider the following scenario.

> Sue is poking and hitting her brother. Her mother says, "Sue, I cannot allow you to poke and hit your brother when you play together. If you poke your brother, you will choose to sit in the corner. It's your choice." Sue says, "Okay," but she continues to poke and hit. Her mother then says, "Sue, you poked your brother. You have made a choice to sit in the corner and not play. Tomorrow you can try again to play correctly with your brother."

Punishment, such as the removal of a reinforcer, should be used as a second choice to reinforcement. Always try to reinforce appropriate behavior before using punishment. Reinforce appropriate behavior that is opposite of the misbehavior. The child cannot act appropriately and misbehave at the same time. Appropriate behavior is incompatible with misbehavior. Let us look at the example of Sue once again.

> The following day Sue's mother says, "Sue, I like the way you and your brother are playing. You are sharing and playing nicely together." Sue says, "I like to play with Jon." Her mother replies, "Because you are playing so well you can play an extra five minutes today."

Sue's mother saw her using appropriate play behavior. Sue was reinforced for displaying appropriate behavior that is incompatible with the poking and hitting behaviors seen earlier. If Sue is rewarded for good playing behavior, this behavior will likely continue. And if Sue is playing well, she cannot misbehave. Therefore, because her mother reinforces her good playing behavior, she is unlikely to repeat her previous misbehavior.

Giving Time-Out The time-out procedure is another way to reduce inappropriate behavior. Time-out removes the child from other people or rewarding objects. The child is removed from the reinforcing situation (by being placed in the corner or in another room) after he or she misbehaves. To be effective, time-out must be given immediately and without fuss. The length of the time-out should be determined before the child is removed. This time should not exceed five minutes (Baker et al. 1976). Having a clock in the time-out area along with a cardboard clock will help you be explicit about how long the child must remain in time-out. If you tell your child that he or she has five minutes of time-out, you could point to the real clock and show your child the current time. Then, you could point to the cardboard clock with the future time displayed (five minutes later). Finally, you could tell your child that when the real clock reaches the same time as the cardboard clock, time-out will be over.

Remember, this technique means time out from the opportunity to be rewarded (to receive a reinforcer). A separate room, corner, or chair are all effective time-out places. This technique should only be used if the other two methods of ignoring and punishing the misbehavior do not stop the unwanted behavior.

The principles related to the use of time-out are listed below. It is important to adhere to each of these principles as closely as possible when administering time-out. Following each of these guidelines during a single time-out episode will add to the possibility of experiencing success with this consequence.

1. Choose an area for time-out that has minimal distractions so that the child receives no attention or rewards while he or she is in the time-out area.

2. Explain to the child about the time-out in advance. Specify which behaviors are cause for time-out; where time-out is located; how long the time-out will last (a general rule of thumb is one minute for each year of the child's age, up to five minutes; this rule could be flexible depending on the severity of the misbehavior). Give your child expectations about what will happen.

3. A one-warning system may be used when you are ready to administer time-out. You may give your child a choice that if the behavior does not stop then he or she will have chosen time-out.

4. Remain calm while taking your child to the time-out area. Keep your discussions about going to time-out to a minimum. Do not argue with your child about assigning time-out. Use as few words as possible. Say "time-out" or point in the direction of the time-out area.

5. Do not respond to your child while he or she is in the time-out area. Respond only after the designated time has been completed and your child has behaved appropriately.

6. Do not call attention to the incident when time-out is over. If your child has questions about the time-out, respond by giving an explanation that indicates that the child made a choice to go to time-out by choosing misbehavior.

7. After the child has completed time-out, praise or reward the child for appropriate behavior.

Keep in mind that if your child is doing something he or she does not like, your child may use time-out as a means of doing something more reinforcing or to avoid an activity that he or she does not like (e.g., homework, chores, etc.) (Goldstein 1995).

> Carl has a habit of biting his brother whenever they watch television together. Carl's mother and father explain that he is not to bite his brother. Carl continues. The parents now tell him that biting is not appropriate under any circumstances. They show him a picture of this inappropriate behavior with an "X" drawn over it, and tell Carl, "No!" They also clearly state that Carl will be given a three-minute time-out period if he continues biting. Time-out is designated to be a corner in the room clear of all toys or interesting material. Carl continues to bite his brother as they watch their favorite cartoon. Carl's mother immediately says, "Carl, you bit your brother. You have chosen time-out." He begins to cry, and says, "It won't happen again." Mother responds by pointing to the time-out area. Carl goes to time-out. After three minutes, Carl's mother allows him to again watch television. She later praises him for how well he is watching television with his brother.

Only you can decide on the best consequences for a given problem behavior. Remember, use positive reinforcement generously by rewarding good and appropriate behavior. If you find it necessary, remove the reward that keeps your child misbehaving. Many times the payoff (reward) is attention. The child receives attention when misbehavior occurs. Ignoring, removing a reward, or time-out are often effective consequences for preventing and stopping misbehavior.

As stated previously, consequences can be changed to decrease misbehavior. An example of a grandfather interacting with his five-year-old grandchild will illustrate this point (this same situation was described in chapter six, now it is presented with a focus on the consequences used).

> A five-year-old boy taps his grandfather hard whenever he wants his attention. The tap is not extremely forceful or harmful but it is annoying. The grandfather explains to the boy, through demonstration, that tapping hard is not appropriate. He tells him he will not listen to him or look at him if he is tapped in this manner. The boy will receive attention only if he gains his grandfather's eye contact and uses proper ways to signal him. The grandfather also uses the consequence of ignoring the boy if he taps him hard to ask for something or to express a need. He only responds to an emergency. The grandfather also decides to teach his grandson the appropriate skills needed to gain the attention of others (e.g., waving his hand in the direction of his grandfather).

Whenever the child practices these skills or uses appropriate methods, he is given positive consequences and is rewarded for his behavior with praise at the moment and given stickers at the end of the day. In time, the child not only decreases his hitting behavior, but increases his use of the new skills he learned for getting others' attention.

Remember to replace the inappropriate behaviors with alternative behaviors. This will enable the child to practice appropriate ways of behaving. At times it may seem difficult to apply the needed consequences consistently because of the nature of the hearing loss. But in order for your plan to work, consequences must be enforced consistently. Long-term gains far outweigh short-term displeasure.

All of the examples given illustrate the three important points to remember when making a plan to change deaf children's behavior:

1. Examine the antecedents in relation to your child's hearing loss. Is the setting appropriate for your child to receive or give

messages? Is there something in your child's environment that increases the occurrence of a problem behavior because of his or her hearing loss or the manner in which your family communicates?

2. Examine your child's behavior in relation to family communication. Do you, your child, or other family members lack the communication skills needed to discuss your child's wants and needs? Could this bring on the misbehavior? Learning how to communicate in your child's language will help alleviate the problems that communication barriers can cause. Teaching your child appropriate ways to express wants or needs with signing, gestures, pictures, etc., may ease the frustration. Also, annoying behaviors may result directly from the impact of your child's condition (e.g., making loud noises). Simple demonstration or explanation sometimes alleviates these problem behaviors.

3. Do not assume that your child can make the connection between your rules and the behaviors you deem appropriate or the consequences you give. You must make explicit connections between behaviors and consequences. Demonstrate for your child before and following episodes of misbehavior all that is important to the situation. Be sure your child understands the connections. Visual and tactile methods often provide the proof a deaf child needs to make a logical connection between behaviors and consequences. The use of logical consequences can also help your child to understand these connections (see chapter seven). And always use positive consequences. A hug, smile, or praise could be all that your child needs to behave appropriately.

PARENT AND CHILD

The following stories illustrate certain problem behaviors shown by deaf children. Analyze each situation. See if your analysis matches the A-B-C pattern given.

Charlie is really driving us crazy. Every time he plays with neighborhood children, he bites them. We are afraid that soon he will have no one to play with.

A Antecedents	B Behavior	C Consequences
Charlie and a neighbor child are playing with toys. Charlie wants a toy the other child is playing with, but the child refuses to give the toy to Charlie.	Charlie bites the child.	The other child cries and gives Charlie the toy he wants. The child runs home to tell his parents about the incident.

I'm so frustrated with Sam. When I work with him using language blocks, he yells and makes horrible noises. The class is disrupted too much. I allow him to use the color board until he calms down.

A Antecedents	B Behavior	C Consequences
A teacher brings sign language blocks to Sam. Sam hates working on language skills.	Sam screams, yells, and makes noises. The teacher is irritated and the class is disrupted.	The teacher gives Sam the color board so he can calm down. He is able to avoid working on language. He likes to color.

Joanie is now so much better when going to bed. I told her I would read her one story each night as long as she is dressed and in bed by nine o'clock. Boy, she loves stories.

A Antecedents	B Behavior	C Consequences
Joanie's mother reminds her to be in bed by nine o'clock, ready for storytime.	Joanie gets ready for bed and is in bed by nine o'clock.	Joanie's mother comes in the room and sees her in bed. She reads one of Joanie's favorite stories.

The next section contains examples of parents who have used the A-B-C pattern successfully with their deaf and hard of hearing children. First, the parents analyzed the behavior using the A-B-C pattern. Second, they decided to change the antecedents and consequences to decrease and/or stop the misbehavior.

Lois is a seven-year-old hard of hearing child who does not comply with her parents' wishes. For example, she refuses to do some household chores when asked. The parents decide to use the A-B-C pattern to analyze her misbehavior. The results of their analysis are as follows:

A Antecedents	B Behavior	C Consequences
Lois's mother requests that Lois clean up her room on a Saturday afternoon.	Lois shakes her head and closes her eyes. She tries to leave the room, refusing to do her chore.	Lois is kept in her room until she does the chore.

After analyzing this behavior pattern, Lois's parents discover that they can change the antecedents and consequences of her behavior. They believe that changing these parts of the pattern will reduce Lois's noncompliant behavior. The parents decide to arrange a designated time each week for Lois to do her chores. This time will be arranged on a consistent basis (the same time each week). Also, Lois will do her chores before she plays. The antecedent (mother making a request while the child was playing) helped prevent Lois from behaving appropriately. Also, the parents believe it is important to keep Lois from playing (consequence) until her chore is completed. Lois will remain in the house until she follows the request. They believe a positive consequence should be given when Lois behaves appropriately. They decide to reinforce Lois with extra playtime when she completes her expected work.

David is a three-year-old deaf youngster. He has developed a habit of biting other children. His biting behavior occurs when he is playing or working beside children in his preschool group. David's father is frustrated with his son's behavior. The father becomes concerned when another parent tells her child to bite David back to show him how it feels. David's father realizes something must be done. He decides to use the A-B-C pattern. This pattern is a summary of several patterns observed over time.

David's father reviews the information gathered from the A-B-C pattern. He decides that the consequences to David's behavior must

A Antecedents	B Behavior	C Consequences
The biting occurs when another child is using something David wants (a crayon, swing at the playground, etc.). David first attempts to get another child's attention by biting.	David bites the children at the playground and in preschool.	The children ignore David's attempts at getting what he wants. The children cry, scream, and sometimes hit David. An adult comes to the other child's rescue. David gets what he wants while the attention is on the other child.

be altered immediately. David's father and his teacher designate a time-out area for David during the preschool period. David is shown explicitly that biting is not appropriate through demonstration of inappropriate biting behaviors and appropriate replacement behaviors.

David's father also draws a picture of a younger child biting another child and indicates his disapproval. This picture is placed in the time-out area. Every time David is seen biting another child, David is placed immediately in time-out for three minutes. The adult shows David the picture of the limit and firmly shakes his or her head no. David's father believes that his son is not aware of appropriate behaviors for expressing his wants. David responds quickly without thinking about his behavior. Reviewing the antecedents, his father sees that David does try to get the child's attention first before biting. He decides to teach his child appropriate ways of communicating his wants and needs to others. In

addition to using the time-out consequence for his son's misbehavior, David's father knows that he must also reinforce David for appropriate behaviors towards other children.

POINTS TO REMEMBER

1. Limit setting provides the fundamental groundwork for the day-to-day management of behavior. Sometimes you may find that your child continually displays problem behavior or that a specific problem behavior needs special attention.

2. All children are capable of displaying annoying behaviors that prove troublesome or stressful to parents. You must decide which behaviors you want to limit and change.

3. All parents try to change, modify, or limit their children's behavior. What determines success is whether or not you use a plan to change behavior.

4. The principles of behavior modification are that your child will tend to repeat a behavior that brings a pleasurable or good outcome, and your child will avoid behaviors that do not produce a favorable outcome.

5. The most difficult aspect of changing behavior is consistency. Following a plan helps make what you do clear to you and your child.

6. The A-B-C pattern provides a framework for consistency by making you aware of

   Antecedents: the setting in which the behavior takes place;

   Behavior: the specific behavior that occurs;

   Consequences: the actions that follow the behavior in that particular setting.

7. No two children behave alike. Each child is unique. Hearing loss does not make your child different; it adds to his or her uniqueness.

8. Hearing loss has little negative effect on the success of the A-B-C pattern. In fact, this pattern is particularly effective with deaf and hard of hearing children because it does not rely on spoken

English for its success. However, even though you may use the pattern to modify behavior, it is important to effectively communicate to your child the behavior that needs to change, the behavior wanted, and the consequences that will follow either kind of behavior.

9. Problem behaviors are successful ways your child has learned to get what he or she wants from the environment.

10. You can prevent or stop a misbehavior by changing the setting.

11. Consequences, for the most part, involve rewards (pleasant outcomes) and punishments (unpleasant outcomes). The three most frequently used consequences to decrease problem behavior are ignoring a behavior, punishing a behavior, and giving time-out.

12. To stop or prevent a misbehavior from occurring, you must remove the reward that keeps the child misbehaving. Many times the payoff (reward) is attention. The child receives attention when misbehavior occurs.

13. Applying the A-B-C pattern to deaf children's behavior is done in the same manner as with hearing children. You must, however, examine the A-B-C pattern from your child's point of view.

14. Replace the inappropriate behaviors with alternative behaviors. This will enable your child to practice appropriate behavior. Reward your child for appropriate behavior.

15. The nature of the hearing loss may make it difficult to apply the needed consequences consistently. In order for your plan to work, consequences must be enforced consistently. Long-term gains far outweigh short-term displeasure.

■ Activities For Practice

1. Take ten minutes to describe an interaction you have had with your child that involved a misbehavior. Describe your child's specific behavior and how you responded to that behavior. Finally, describe how your child reacted to your response. How do you feel about the interaction? Was your response effective?

Your Child's Behavior	Your Response	Your Child's Reaction
_____	_____	_____
_____	_____	_____
_____	_____	_____
_____	_____	_____
_____	_____	_____
_____	_____	_____

Comments

_____

_____

2. If you are not satisfied with the outcome of the interaction described in Activity 1, analyze this interaction using the A-B-C pattern. If you are satisfied with the outcome of the interaction, then choose another interaction involving misbehavior that you would like to analyze.

A Antecedents	B Behavior	C Consequences
_____	_____	_____
_____	_____	_____
_____	_____	_____
_____	_____	_____
_____	_____	_____
_____	_____	_____

3. Read the following story. Underline the parts of the story you believe to be the Antecedents (A), Behavior (B), and Consequences (C), and label them A, B, C, accordingly. Check your responses against those in the Feedback and Answers section. If your analysis was different, look back through the pages of chapter eight that describe the A-B-C pattern.

Sam is twelve years old. Sam often demands that his mother give or buy him something or let him go somewhere. Sam asks these things of his mother in a matter-of-fact way, both in his home and in public. When his mother does not give him what he wants immediately, Sam repeats his requests louder and louder. Eventually, he gets very angry and shouts and screams. When he is this angry he also throws things. These episodes occur less often when his father is present. But his demanding behavior is more intense when he is in front of company or in a public place. His mother reacts to such episodes by begging and pleading with Sam not to cause a scene. She also shouts and screams at him to be quiet. Sometimes she gets tired and gives in more readily in public places to avoid embarrassment.

Write your own comments in the space below.

_____

_____

_____

_____

_____

_____

_____

_____

4. Read the following situation. Use the A-B-C pattern provided below to analyze this situation. Based on your analysis, what do you think about Johnny's behavior? Write your comments in the spaces below the pattern.

You are the parent of Johnny, a deaf eight-year-old. Johnny is supposed to go to his room at 4:00 p.m., when he gets home from school, to do his homework. Johnny does not like to do his homework. His teacher says that she has not received his homework for the past week. You decide to check in on Johnny and find him watching cartoons at 4:00 p.m. in his room and his homework sheets are torn up in the wastebasket.

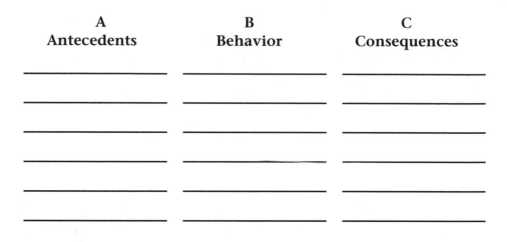

A Antecedents	B Behavior	C Consequences
_____	_____	_____
_____	_____	_____
_____	_____	_____
_____	_____	_____
_____	_____	_____
_____	_____	_____

Putting It All Together

You have now reached the final chapters of this book. Thus far, we have discussed feelings about hearing loss, dealing with those feelings, the importance of communication, the behavior of deaf children, and how to set limits and handle misbehavior. A great deal of information has been presented. You may not retain all the information discussed, but you can refer back to the information and use it as a general guideline for future interactions with your child.

In this chapter, we will review several points and help you apply these points so as to enhance the interactions between you and your child. We will give you guidelines to help you develop a personal plan of action a plan for working with your behavior and your child's behavior.

This chapter does not follow the same format as the previous chapters. It is now time to put the information you have read to use to put it all together.

In order to get the most from this chapter, you must decide where to begin. Use specific information relative to your own family situation. For example, perhaps you suspect that your feelings are interfering with how effectively you handle your child's behavior. Maybe you would profit from reviewing the section on recognizing your feelings, paying close attention to and outlining how to cope and work with your feelings. If you are interested in exploring the effectiveness of your family's communication, then concentrate on the area of this chapter that discusses family communication. If you have a difficult time developing general rules in your household, you may want to review closely the section on setting limits on behavior.

You have mastered valuable information about you and your child while reading this book. It is now time to put that knowledge to use. At the end of this chapter, there are worksheets to assist you in those areas where you have the greatest need.

PROBLEM SOLVING

You can improve family interactions by treating them as problem-solving situations. Problem solving involves six steps: (1) identifying the problem area; (2) describing or discussing your feelings about the problem; (3) determining your goal or what you want to happen; (4) deciding what is stopping you from getting to that goal; (5) brainstorming and considering strategies needed to get you to your goal; and (6) implementing a plan and evaluating its effectiveness.

Let us look at an example of how you can use the problem-solving techniques with your child. Suppose your child does not comply with your requests. You become very frustrated when this happens. Your goal is to get your child to obey when you make requests; however, your emotions may be an obstacle that prevents you from achieving your goal. A strategy for overcoming this obstacle would be to discuss what you want done at a time when you are calm. You can evaluate the effectiveness of this strategy by measuring how often your child follows your directions when you present them in a calm manner.

The personal plan you develop should follow this general problem-solving approach. In the future, you can use the approach as a step-by-step strategy to solve a variety of problems. For example, when you are having a problem, you can say the problem-solving process out loud—"I'm having a problem with (state the problem). I'm feeling (describe the feeling[s]). What can I do? (brainstorm your ideas). I could _____, or I could _____, or I could _____. I think that _____ is the best idea, so I'll try this first (implement your plan and then evaluate it) (adapted from Greenberg 1990, pp. 13–14).

Evaluating Your Plan's Effectiveness

An important part of the problem-solving approach is evaluating your strategy. Any time you decide on a problem-solving strategy, you need to determine if the strategy works. One way to do this is to ask yourself if you feel better about what is happening, or if the situation is better as a result of what you have done. You can review the plan to evaluate the success of this strategy. This is a crucial part of solving problems. Let us look at the problem-solving method again to emphasize how important evaluation is in determining its success.

1. Problem: Billy throws a tantrum when asked to put away his toys.

2. Description of Feelings: I am discouraged because this behavior happens so frequently. I am getting angry at Billy.

3. Goal: To stop Billy's tantrum behaviors.

4. Obstacles: When Billy throws a tantrum, I give in. I get so angry I lose control.

5. Strategy: Use the A-B-C pattern to help stop tantrum behavior. Also, I need to calm down before I respond with a consequence.

A Antecedent	B Behavior	C Consequences
Billy is in the play-room. He is told to put away his toys.	Billy throws a tantrum.	Billy must leave the playroom immediately. Billy's play period is taken away.

6. Evaluation: Tantrum behaviors did not decrease after one week. I need to change my strategy or part of my strategy. I will change the consequences to two minutes in the time-out room. I will implement my strategy as soon as possible. I will reevaluate this new strategy after one week.

The three worksheets that follow present information on the three problem areas discussed throughout this book: dealing with strong feelings, evaluating family communication, and setting limits and managing behavior. You can use one or all three worksheets depending on your needs.

Worksheet 1: Dealing with Your Feelings

1. Before you work on behavior, either your own or your child's, you need to be aware of your feelings. Your feelings are reactions to past or present situations or what you believe may occur in the future. Feelings may stem from painful experiences that happened years ago or from present experiences, such as dealing with your child's behavior. The following statements address aspects of your feelings about your child's hearing loss. Becoming aware of your feelings and controlling them will help you make better decisions.

   Check those statements that apply to your feelings about the diagnosis of your child's hearing loss.

   a. _____ I have strong feelings about my child's hearing loss.

   b. _____ I wish over and over again that my child could hear.

   c. _____ Many times I still feel angry about those days when my child was first being diagnosed as having a hearing loss.

   d. _____ I get upset about the way the doctors, audiologists, and other medical staff handled the situation.

   e. _____ I am frustrated over the entire situation in dealing with my child's condition.

   f. _____ List any other feelings you may have regarding the diagnosis of your child's hearing loss:

   _____

   _____

   _____

   The statements listed above make explicit certain feelings you may have about the diagnosis of your child's hearing loss. If you checked one or more of the statements or added comments concerning your feelings, it is important not to ignore these feelings. Dealing with the feelings can help you overcome them and help you cope with life changes that occur as a result of having a child with a hearing loss. Continue with the next series of statements and develop your plan for coping with the feelings that you are experiencing.

2. Dealing with hearing loss on a daily basis, I find that

   a. _____ I am frightened when I think of what will happen to my child in the world.

   b. _____ I get upset when I see hearing children playing or working together.

   c. _____ Sometimes I get angry and upset when trying to discipline my child because of our communication difficulties.

   d. _____ I am tired of trying to communicate with my child each day. We never seem to get anywhere.

   e. _____ I often feel sad when my child becomes frustrated and cannot understand because of communication problems.

f. _____ At times I feel overwhelmed because of the responsibility of taking care of my family and looking after the needs of my child.

g. _____ List any other feelings that come up because of your child's hearing loss:

_____

_____

_____

Your responses to the previous statements describe feelings that are common. Parents with deaf and hard of hearing children report having these same feelings from time to time. Do not ignore them. The following section will help you to develop a plan to deal with some of the feelings you have because of the diagnosis of your child's hearing loss or what the hearing loss means to you and your family.

3. List some of your feelings that frequently occur.

Example: Sadness about my child's hearing loss. Why did this happen?

_____

_____

_____

_____

_____

4. List ways you have used to deal with your feelings about the diagnosis of your child's hearing loss or what the hearing loss means to you and your family.

Example: When feeling depressed about how deafness affects my family, I watch television, sleep, or do work around the house.

_____

_____

_____

_____

_____

5. Have these ways of coping worked? Yes _____   No _____
If no, list alternative ways to deal with your feelings.

Coping Strategy	Result	Alternative Ways of Coping
Example: When I feel depressed, I usually watch television and forget about it.	The depression does not lessen.	Talk to my spouse, a close friend, or another parent of a deaf or hard of hearing child about my feelings.
————————	————————	————————
————————	————————	————————
————————	————————	————————
————————	————————	————————
————————	————————	————————

6. Fill in the blank: I get very upset about my child's behavior
   when ————————————

   Example: My child closes his eyes when I am talking to him.

   ————————————————————————————

   ————————————————————————————

   ————————————————————————————

   ————————————————————————————

7. Describe how you typically deal with strong feelings.

   Example: When my child looks away when I talk to him, I hold his face until he looks at me.

   ————————————————————————————

   ————————————————————————————

   ————————————————————————————

   ————————————————————————————

   ————————————————————————————

   ————————————————————————————

8. Do these ways of coping work? Yes _____   No _____
   If no, list alternative ways of dealing with your feelings.

Example: When my child misbehaves and I am feeling very angry, I can wait until I get calm (by counting to five, by thinking positive thoughts) before I try to communicate with my son.

_____

_____

_____

_____

_____

_____

Continue to evaluate whether your coping strategies work in helping you deal with your feelings.

Worksheet 2: Developing Rules

Perhaps you need to develop a list of clear and consistent rules. The following plan will help you prepare or improve a rule system in your home. Remember to list rules in a positive way.

1. What general rules do you want your child to obey at home?

   Example: Use polite language in the home.

   _____

   _____

   _____

   _____

2. Check the effectiveness of your rules by completing the list below (adapted from Webster-Stratton and Herbert 1994, p. 179).

   _____ The rules are necessary.
   _____ They are stated in a positive way.
   _____ They are stated in simple terms and are visually posted through statements, drawings, and/or photographs.
   _____ They are fair.
   _____ My child understands them.
   _____ I (and my partner or spouse) apply these rules fairly.

3. How will you reward your child for following your main rules? Use the space provided below to list your thoughts concerning use of rewards.

   Example: My child will be verbally praised throughout the day and will earn an extra privilege (e.g., spend an extra half hour at the park).

   _____

   _____

   _____

   _____

4. What will you do the first time your child breaks these main rules?

   Example: Remind my child about the rule, warn my child, etc.

   _____

   _____

_____

_____

_____

5. What will you do the second time your child breaks the main rules?

  Example: Take away privileges; make the child stay inside the house for a half hour; etc.

_____

_____

_____

_____

_____

6. What rules do you need to set for specific times of the day? (State rules in a positive way.) As needed, complete the checklist presented in #2 for each specific set of rules you list below.

Play Period	Dinnertime	Bedtime	Other (Specify)
_____	_____	_____	_____
_____	_____	_____	_____
_____	_____	_____	_____
_____	_____	_____	_____
_____	_____	_____	_____

7. What will you do when your child follows the specific rules in your home?

_____

_____

_____

_____

_____

8. What will you do the first time your child breaks these specific rules?

  Example: Remind her about the rule, give a warning, etc.

Play Period	Dinnertime	Bedtime	Other (Specify)
_____	_____	_____	_____
_____	_____	_____	_____
_____	_____	_____	_____
_____	_____	_____	_____
_____	_____	_____	_____

9. What will you do the second time your child breaks a specific rule?

   Example: Take away privileges; child loses a portion of playtime.

Play Period	Dinnertime	Bedtime	Other (Specify)
_____	_____	_____	_____
_____	_____	_____	_____
_____	_____	_____	_____
_____	_____	_____	_____
_____	_____	_____	_____

10. Did you generally respond to your child in the way you wanted?
    Yes _____   No _____

11. Did you clearly communicate the rules to your child?
    Yes _____   No _____

12. Did you follow up the rule with the appropriate consequence consistently (every time) when your child broke the rule?
    Yes _____   No _____

13. Are your set consequences (pleasant/unpleasant) helping your child follow the rules?
    Yes _____   No _____

14. Review your overall plan. Do you need to change all or part of your plan? If so, write down the kinds of changes you need to make.

    _____

    _____

    _____

    _____

Worksheet 3: A Plan for Evaluating Family Communication

1. What are your beliefs about family communication in relation to your child's hearing loss?

   _____

   _____

   _____

   _____

   _____

2. What mode of communication do you use consistently in your home? (Complete for each family member.)

   a. Indicate the type of communication below:
      _____ strictly oral
      _____ strictly manual
      _____ simultaneous communication
      _____ gestures and speech
      _____ cued speech
      _____ other (specify)

   b. If you use some form of sign language in your home, what type do you use?
      _____ American Sign Language (ASL)
      _____ Signing Exact English (SEE II)
      _____ Signed English
      _____ Pidgin Sign English (PSE)
      _____ Other (specify)

3. On a scale from 1 to 5 (1 being least effective and 5 being most effective), how would you rate your effectiveness in using the above system in communicating your thoughts and feelings to your deaf child? Complete ratings for each family member as each person may use a different communication system.

Name of Family Member	Communication System	Rating
_____	_____	_____
_____	_____	_____
_____	_____	_____

_____   _____   _____

_____   _____   _____

_____   _____   _____

4. If an individual scored 1 to 3 on the above scale, describe a plan to increase communication effectiveness with your child. A plan can include ways to learn how better to communicate visually. These ways can include taking sign language classes, discussing techniques with deaf adults or adolescents, developing nonverbal communication skills, increasing interaction with deaf and hard of hearing adults, practicing eye contact, using physical touch, utilizing visual images or pictures during interactions, and using videotapes and books to learn about effective communication with deaf people.

Plan for _____

_____

_____

_____

_____

_____

Plan for _____

_____

_____

_____

_____

_____

Plan for _____

_____

_____

_____

_____

_____

5. Please evaluate yourself in relation to your ability to help your child visually attend to your communication. Choose a ten-minute period of time when you will interact alone with your child while discussing something that he or she needs to do in your home (e.g., household chores, a family activity). Videotape this interaction, if possible, to receive immediate feedback about the interaction.

   After reviewing the videotape or thinking back on your interaction, rate yourself on a scale of 1 to 5 (1 being least effective; 5 being most effective) on how well you followed the guidelines below in effectively communicating with your child.

Guidelines	Rating
Gaining your child's visual attention.	_____
Maintaining your child's visual attention during communication.	_____
Allowing your child to orient visually to the object of discussion.	_____
Allowing your child to orient back to you and to the communication process after looking at the object.	_____
Allowing your child to "lead" the communication as much as possible; following your child's leads.	_____

Now comment on your strengths and the areas you will need to improve upon based on your experiences with this interaction. Remember, it is important to continue to monitor and evaluate your progress in developing effective communication skills with your child.

_____

_____

_____

_____

_____

Meeting Your Child's Communication Needs

Being the hearing parent of a deaf child produces many concerns and questions about the future. What effect will hearing loss have on your child's life? How will this condition influence and change your life and the development of your family? Will your child be able to have a good life? Can your child find happiness? How can you gather the information you need concerning hearing loss?

Throughout this book, we have concentrated on learning more about your feelings, your family's manner of communication, your behavior, your child's behavior, behavior management, and your ways of coping with your situation. Gathering information about hearing loss and how it affects your child and your life is one way of coping. This strategy enables you to begin understanding hearing loss and its implications and helps you develop expectations for you and your child.

In this chapter we will examine several areas deemed important in meeting the needs of deaf children: technological assistance, educational placement, quality interpreting services, and the Deaf community and culture. The information provided in this chapter may also help you locate the specific information you need to cope with your unanswered questions. Each area is examined briefly. Sources relative to each area are provided in the resource and suggested reading lists at the end of the book. These lists can be helpful in your quest for better understanding of hearing loss and related issues.

TECHNOLOGICAL ASSISTANCE

On July 26, 1990, President George Bush signed into law the Americans with Disabilities Act (ADA). This Act covers the rights of a broad range of individuals, protecting them from discrimination in the public and private sectors of our society (Firth 1994). The major portions of the ADA have been in effect since 1992 and we are seeing their effects in such changes as TTY pay phones in major metropolitan airports and television captioning in prominent hotels. The ADA has increased public awareness by propelling disability-related issues to the forefront of American public policy. Therefore, technological advances will be forthcoming as deaf and hard of hearing people demand access to new technological services.

The way our society communicates is rapidly changing. Computers, multimedia, and interactive services have created a revolution in the way we exchange information and obtain services. The lesson of the telephone and television was invaluable to the deaf community (Firth 1994). The ADA, with its guarantees of equal access, will continue to have a huge impact on deaf people with respect to the ways technology can help them gain access to information in our society. This section will look at technology as it relates to the support services available to deaf children and their families.

Hearing Aids

Many people consider the use of hearing aids as vital to educating and socializing deaf children. Relatives or friends often erroneously believe that deaf children can become hearing people as soon as they are fitted with hearing aids (Meadow 1980). But hearing aids are not a substitute for hearing; they will not restore your child's ability to hear. A hearing aid only makes sounds louder; it does not correct hearing (Rodda and Grove 1987). Even with the best hearing aid, children benefit differently, depending on the nature of their loss. Some children may hear some speech sounds, but other children may not hear any speech at all. Some children with hearing losses can use hearing aids to pick up environmental sounds (Deyo and Gelzer 1991). Still others do not benefit from using a hearing aid at all. Most deaf children, however, have some residual hearing that can be amplified (Luterman 1986; Scheetz 1993).

The type of hearing loss your child has will determine how the hearing aid can help. If a family chooses to outfit their child with a hearing aid, an individual evaluation must be scheduled to determine which type of hearing aid will be most effective (Scheetz 1993). In one case, a hearing aid will enable a child to hear only very loud sounds. In another case, a hearing aid may permit words or phrases to be heard. The type of hearing loss will determine which hearing aid is best for your child and what sounds will be made louder. A hearing aid is basically a microphone and amplifier that are attached to an earmold that must be properly placed in the ear. Hearing aids exist in a variety of shapes and sizes. These range from a radio transmission system the size of a small box that is typically used in the classroom all the way down to a small aid that is worn inside the ear (Rodda and Grove 1987).

Keep in mind that your child may not like to wear the hearing aid. The earmold will feel strange in the ear. Your child may hear sounds for the first time and may find them confusing. Hence, the aids may be uncomfortable. They may also amplify sound in a way that is painful (Mahshie 1995). Your child's beliefs or feelings about hearing aids need to be addressed. Children who benefit from hearing aids typically accept wearing them (Mahshie 1995). If a hearing aid is appropriate for your child, it will aid hearing only if it is used as a consistent and integral part of your child's life, as a daily routine. If used haphazardly or inconsistently, the aid may add confusion since what is picked up from the environment may change from day to day.

Several elements contribute to the effectiveness of hearing aids for your child (adapted from Parreca 1987):

1. The appropriateness of the hearing aid in meeting your child's needs;

2. Your child's attitude toward wearing hearing aids;

3. Your child's motivation in learning how to use the aids;

4. Your adjustment to the hearing loss;

5. Your understanding about what hearing aids *can* do (intensify some sounds in the environment) and what they *can't* do (correct or restore hearing).

Additionally, parents should receive an orientation on how to use hearing aids and get information they can pass on to their children. The orientation should provide the following information (adapted from Scheetz 1993, pp. 266–267):

1. How to insert, remove, and clean the earmold;

2. How to utilize the on-off switch, the volume control, the telephone switch, and the tone control;

3. The type of batteries the aid uses, where to purchase them, and how to change them;

4. What the device can and cannot do to improve communication;

5. What the user's communication abilities and limitations may be with the hearing aid.

Cochlear Implants

Cochlear implants are electronic devices that bypass the nonfunctioning inner ear hair cells and convert sounds to electric impulses. Implantees must undergo a surgical procedure to receive the implant. The effectiveness of this procedure depends on a number of factors such as the nature of the hearing loss and individual needs. The decision to have an implant is determined by specific criteria and thorough evaluation.

The implant does not restore sounds like regular hearing but rather provides a series of sounds that resemble beeps, buzzes and whistles. A person can then encode and provide meaning to them. The implant surgery involves placing an internal coil under the skin behind the ear and a stimulating electrode directly within the inner ear or cochlea (Epstein 1987).

This procedure is highly controversial. Some believe that the procedure is a technological advance to be considered by parents of deaf children. Others, such as the National Association of the Deaf (NAD) and other organizations of deaf people around the world, point to the lack of scientific evidence to justify the highly experimental nature of this surgery for young children (Lane, as cited in Mahshie 1995). The following statements are representative of the arguments for and against parents choosing the cochlear implant procedure for their young children:

A child for whom this technology is deemed appropriate will receive the maximum understanding of sounds and this will allow for better access to oral language and environmental cues.

"My subjective impression has been that the most 'functional implantees'—those who can communicate best and seem to be the happiest—are those who have added an implant to a full complement of skills for coping with deafness—including a deaf-positive attitude and acceptance of sign language" (Woodcock 1992, p. 153).

This technique is a barbaric one that intrudes on the rights of each deaf child since he or she can't be a part of the decision about whether or not to have this surgery. Also, the insertion of the cochlear implant eliminates any existing residual hearing by destroying the fibers at the end of the auditory nerve (Lane 1994).

Telecommunication Devices

Telecommunication devices for the deaf (TDDs) were originally known as teletypewriters (TTYs), and most adults in the Deaf community still call them TTYs. These machines have the appearance of a small typewriter that can be used with regular telephone handsets to allow deaf people to communicate with each other and with hearing individuals. The TTY is made up of a typewriter-like keyboard, a telephone coupler, and some form of visual display where words are typed via TTY tones (Scheetz 1993).

With the passage of the ADA, relay services have been established in most major cities across the United States. A relay service involves the use of a telephone operator with a TTY who serves as a link between a deaf person with a TTY and a hearing person without one (Dolnick 1993). Relay services have 1-800 numbers and are used at no charge to the calling party. You can call 1-800-555-1212 to locate the relay number in your area or check in the inside cover of your local telephone book for the relay number.

Also, because of the ADA, hotels are starting to have TTYs, captioned television, and signaling devices such as fire alarms with flashing lights available for their deaf patrons.

Signaling Devices

Signaling devices use light (regular or strobe) or vibrations to assist deaf individuals in attending to different environmental sounds such as the telephone or doorbell ringing, the baby crying, and smoke or fire alarms (Scheetz 1993). Wake-up alarms, telephone/doorbell signalers, beepers, emergency warning devices, and emergency alarm devices have also been developed for deaf and hard of hearing people.

Television and Movie Captioning

For many years, before the closed captioning of network television programs became a reality, television was not a source of entertainment or information for most deaf people. The thrill that deaf people get from closed captioned television programs can be likened to the experience hearing people had when television was a novelty in the 1950s (Schragle and Bateman 1994).

In order to see the captions on a television program or videotape, a television must have a caption decoder. Up until 1993, the decoders

were attached to the television. All new television sets 13 inches or larger made after July 1993 have built-in decoders so that captioning is more readily available to everyone. Additionally, some videotapes are open captioned, so they do not require a decoder to view. Deaf people are now gaining more access to information and a greater sense of independence as they take advantage of captioning technology.

Parents should be aware that the educational benefits of captioning are tremendous (Schragle and Bateman 1994). For instance, reading the captions during a television news program supplements the newspaper and can help build English vocabulary. However, the quality and readability of captioning needs to improve. The words and sentences on the screen appear and disappear very quickly. The captions are like subtitles in foreign films. And, while captioning enhances understanding of television programming, the complexities of written English still pose obstacles (Higgins and Nash 1987). Children who enjoy reading will probably benefit the most from watching captioned television. Some parents of young children report that captioning encourages interest in reading (Deyo and Gelzer 1991).

Electronic Mail (E-mail)

With the advent of the computer age, many homes and offices have personal computers that have the capacity for electronic mail (e-mail) on the Internet. This technological advance has afforded deaf individuals the opportunity to converse with each other or with hearing persons using the e-mail system. E-mail has augmented the TTY as a potential communication tool for all members of our technological society.

Telephone Amplifiers

Telephone listening devices increase the loudness of sound coming through the telephone. These devices can be used with or without hearing aids (Scheetz 1993).

EDUCATIONAL PLACEMENT

The type of school environment has been a major issue of conflict in educating deaf children (Mertens 1989). It has historically been related to issues in communication (Quigley and Kretschmer 1982). Many times parents choose the education placement for their child based on the type of communication method used in the home. Specifically, if you decide on an oral communication approach, you might seek out a school placement that uses an oral approach for intervention. If you choose to use sign language in the home, then you will most likely choose an educational placement that emphasizes a manual method as an integral part of your child's school experience. When choosing an educational environment for your child, your family's communication mode, your perceptions about hearing loss, and your philosophy of education will all directly influence the educational setting you select for your child (Scheetz 1993).

Residential Schools

Residential schools can be found in the public and private sectors. A residential school provides both educational and living facilities for deaf students, with few or no provisions for integration with hearing students (Quigley and Kretschmer 1982). At any one time, approximately 30 percent of deaf children are attending one of the 81 state and private residential schools in the United States (Schildroth and Hotto 1996). In most programs, the children spend weekends at home with their families. These schools offer a variety of educational, social, and recreational programs for deaf children. Overall, these programs are designed with the deaf child in mind and employ staff and teachers who have been specifically trained in deaf education (Scheetz 1993). The communication approach most widely used in the residential schools involves types of sign language. Some schools, however, do use an oral approach.

Day Schools

These programs can also be found in the public and private sectors. Day schools are usually located in large populated areas. They are schools that have been established to accommodate deaf students who live at home (Scheetz 1993). Students go to school with deaf students only. Students attend the school during regular daytime hours and return home after program hours.

Day Classes

Day classes are usually located in a public school and provide some degree of integration and mainstreaming of deaf students with hearing students (Quigley and Kretschmer 1982). The classes are usually self-contained, and all students in the class are deaf. Generally, they are located in public schools where the majority of children are hearing (Scheetz 1993). Children can participate in a variety of activities with hearing peers such as lunch, physical education, and certain academic subjects, depending on their needs.

Mainstreamed Programs

Mainstreamed programs involve placing the deaf child in a classroom with hearing children. The extent to which this occurs depends upon the child's academic abilities and way of communicating. In this type of program it is important to consider the availability of support services for the child, such as interpreters, tutors, and note-takers, when planning for your child's mainstreaming experience. You must ensure that your child is having his or her educational needs met appropriately in the mainstream setting.

Possible Restrictions on Educational Choices

Some factors may limit the educational options available to you. The area in which you live may affect your choice of educational placements or may limit your options. For example, a family living in a heavily populated metropolitan area may have access to many services, but a family living in a rural area may have far fewer educational options. The relatively low incidence of hearing loss in the population (approximately 1 in 1,000 births [Paul and Quigley 1990]) suggests that only those school systems that serve a large population will be able to provide enough support services to adequately meet the needs of deaf children. Budget cuts and funding constraints will also help to determine the kinds of programming and services available. You need to be alert to these shifts of funding or attitudes concerning the provision of services in order to make informed decisions (Davis 1986). Also, the fact many state residential schools for deaf children have closed in recent years will affect some parents' decision making in this area.

The American Society for Deaf Children, a national organization representing 20,000 parents, friends and professionals, expresses strong opinions about the placement of deaf children. They have asked parents to fight against any predetermined formula for placement that runs the risk of disregarding individual educational needs (Mahshie 1995). The right school placement varies from child to child, family to family, and area to area (McArthur 1982). You need to objectively evaluate which is the best placement for your child. Keep in mind that you need not make this decision alone. Deaf adults, other parents of deaf children, and professionals and organizations that work with deaf individuals can all offer you information that will aid in your decision making (see appendix 3 for a checklist of questions for you to use when evaluating educational programs for your child).

Quality Interpreting Services

Interpreters play a vital role in communication between hearing and deaf individuals. In fact, the most frequently requested support service for members of the Deaf community is a qualified sign language interpreter (Firth 1994). Interpreters working in the educational, medical, legal, social, and rehabilitation settings generally require professional training and national certification (Scheetz 1993). Within the context of the ADA, it is mandated that quality interpreting services be available. Interpreters must provide "effective communication." There are many wonderful and qualified interpreters in the United States today. However, with the demand and open market, sometimes individuals who lack experience in deafness and have problems with sign language fluency are hired as freelancers or from interpreting agencies. Early in 1994, the National Association of the Deaf (NAD) and the Registry of Interpreters for the Deaf (RID) recognized the mounting problems with the delivery of quality interpreting services and declared a nationwide crisis (Firth 1994). Due to the nature of their work, it is critical that interpreters are proficient in their skill area, remain impartial, and serve only as communication facilitators (Scheetz 1993). Most organizations, deaf persons, and parents of deaf children are beginning to request only nationally certified interpreters to provide this vital service.

RID was founded in the United States in 1964. The primary mission of this organization is to provide training, establish standards, and grant certification to those interpreters achieving certain skill

levels, and to offer a registry for those seeking to contact the services of a professional interpreter (Scheetz 1993). Additional information about this organization, including the availability of interpreting services in various locations across the country, types of certification, fee schedules, and location of training programs, can be obtained by contacting RID (see appendix 1 for the address and phone number).

DEAF COMMUNITY AND CULTURE

One needs to distinguish between the physiological condition of hearing loss and the association of deaf people with a language and a culture. A very small number of deaf children are born into the Deaf culture. Most children become enculturated during their teenage years or as adults (Paul and Jackson 1993). The Deaf community is in itself a society. It includes a cross-section of people with differing hearing losses, physical builds, races, religions, intelligence, interests, and values (Rosen 1986). Everyone in this world needs to belong. Deaf people are no different. Many deaf individuals function as "outsiders in a hearing world" (Higgins and Nash 1987). Oftentimes they find themselves treated as a minority similar to other groups (e.g., African Americans, Jews, gays, etc.). In responding to the unique differences between their experiences and those of their hearing friends and family, many deaf people identify themselves as a part of Deaf culture.

A culture is made up of people who have their own language, values, rules of behavior, and traditions (Kannapell 1993). Deaf culture binds the Deaf community together through a shared language— American Sign Language (ASL). This language not only has rules for combining signs but also rules governing eye contact, touching, and the use of facial expressions, all of which are vital components of the language. Common interests and experiences strengthen the bonds of this culture and its identity. There are Deaf communities in metropolitan areas across the United States. The members of these communities participate together in a wide variety of activities, including sports, organizations, and the arts (Higgins and Nash 1987; Lane et al. 1996).

In all societies, people are socialized by communicating cultural norms through language (Higgins and Nash 1987). ASL is the preferred language among the members of the Deaf community (Bienvenu 1991; Christensen, 1990; Goodstein, 1990). Culturally deaf people usually capitalize the *D* in *Deaf* to emphasize their proud and separate identity (Colon 1996).

To be a part of Deaf culture, one must want to be identified with the Deaf community and desire to participate fully in its activities. Hearing loss is not a sufficient condition for membership (Scheetz 1993). For example, if an individual has attended a public school, has primarily resided in an "oral" environment, and is not fluent in sign language, that person most probably views himself as a "hearing" person with a condition that affects his full participation in the hearing world rather than as a deaf person identified with the Deaf community and culture. Whereas, a deaf individual who is fluent in ASL, has attended a residential school, and regularly participates in Deaf community activities most likely would call herself Deaf and a member of the Deaf community and culture.

Members of the Deaf community view deafness as a cultural phenomenon rather than as a handicapping condition. They rarely use the term *hearing impaired*, which implies disability; they prefer the terms *deaf* and *hard of hearing* (Higgins and Nash 1987). The terms *deafness* and *hearing-impaired* have become associated with the medical/pathological view that defines deaf and hard of hearing people as broken human beings. Many deaf and hard of hearing individuals thus find these terms hurtful and objectionable (Jordan 1992).

An illustration of how deaf and hearing people can exist in their cultures side-by-side and view deafness as a cultural phenomenon was found in the Chilmark community on the island of Martha's Vineyard from the eighteenth to the early twentieth centuries. In this community in the 1850s, one in every 150 people was deaf (Groce 1985). In one island village with about five hundred residents, one in twenty-five was deaf. Hearing as well as deaf children on the island learned and used the indigenous sign language. The community used the language as an integral part of their lives—fishermen used sign language to communicate at a distance, and others used it in their churches. The hearing and deaf children on the island grew up inter-acting with each other in a comfortable, natural bilingual/bicultural community (Groce 1985).

In our society, since the issue in dealing with the hearing world is communication, deaf people tend to socialize together more than do people with other conditions. Learning about Deaf culture is vital to deaf children so they can know and understand their own culture. While literature, art, and drama entertain and inspire, they also pre-serve and transfer to the young the values of Deaf culture (Vernon and Andrews 1990). Deaf children need to have Deaf adult and ado-lescent role models to help them develop a healthy self-image (Rodda and Grove 1987). Deaf children traditionally administer the rite of passage to newcomers to the Deaf community rather than adults, as in the hearing world. Since, for the most part, deaf children are born into families with hearing members, this is one culture that is typi-cally handed down, generation to generation, from child to child (Benderly 1990).

It is helpful for parents of deaf children to meet and interact with Deaf adults. Not only can Deaf adults serve as positive role models for deaf children, but they help reassure parents that their children can be productive, successful, contributing individuals in their own community and in the larger society.

The poem on page 154 encapsulates the positive self-image and pride that members of the Deaf community feel about their language and culture. It was written by Maria Grace Okwara (1994), who be-came deaf at the age of nine from the mumps. She went to a residen-tial school and then to a mainstream school. She now has a Bachelors of Arts degree in History from Gallaudet University and a Master of Arts in Bilingual Education and Portuguese Studies from Brown Uni-versity.

The Deaf community and its culture provides an example of how a strong system of social support can transform the lives of many people (Higgins and Nash 1987). The peer support of this system in-fluences the coping abilities and the self-esteem of deaf children, youth, and adults throughout our country. For this and the other rea-sons listed below (adapted from Hafer and Ditman-Richard 1990, p. 16), hearing parents should learn about Deaf culture. This knowl-edge will

1. Enable parents to recognize their child's full potential as an indi-vidual.

2. Help parents realize the importance of deaf role models in the development of their child's self-esteem and sense of identity.

3. Help parents view sign language as an acceptable or even a necessary element of their child's development.

4. Help parents welcome, rather than fear, the role of the Deaf community in their child's life.

5. Enrich the child's and family's life by broadening shared traditions, values, and experiences.

With My Hands I Can . . . .

MARIA GRACE OKWARA

With my hands I can
Fly a plane,
Pluck a guitar,
Shout,
Tell a story,
Cry . . . .

With my hands I can
Frown,
Dance,
Smile,
Take a chance . . . .

Tell me what you can do with your voice?

Reprinted by permission of the author from
Deafness: Life and Culture (NAD, 1994), p. 68.

Chapter 11 | Conclusion

Congratulations! You have completed this book in an effort to gain a better understanding of yourself and your child. By reading the material presented in this book and completing the activities offered, you have taken the opportunity to learn more about hearing loss and its effect on your family. You have examined your feelings about hearing loss, your behavior and your child's behavior, and the interactions between you and your child. In doing so, you have taken a risk to grow as a person and, most especially, as a parent of a deaf child. Looking within yourself is difficult at times, but an important part of growing and understanding is being aware of how your feelings and behavior influence you and your interactions with others.

If the information presented in this book has been difficult for you or has helped bring about unwanted feelings, do not be discouraged. You have made a step toward obtaining information about hearing loss in relation to your family.

Gathering information is an important part of coping. Obtaining information is helpful whether you have just discovered your child's hearing loss or you have had years of experience in dealing with it. In either case, this book has given you information you can use in the future. This book was designed to reach a variety of parents with deaf children of differing ages. You can use this book again and again depending on your specific needs throughout your development as a parent and your child's growing years. You may find that as your child matures you will react differently to the material in this book. Or your thoughts and ideas concerning the activities in each chapter may change.

I hope that this book has been helpful to you and will be helpful to others involved with the care and development of deaf children. Since you have read this book, you are in a unique position to offer your opinions about how this book can be developed to better meet your needs and the needs of other parents of deaf children. You may have ideas, thoughts, or suggestions about how to make the book more useful to you and others like yourself. Please share these thoughts with me. Your statements will be kept in strict confidence. If you have such comments, please complete the form on page 191 and mail it to the address listed on the form.

I hope that this book has in some way touched your life. Without a doubt, gathering the information in writing this book, especially my contact with parents of deaf children and professionals who work with these children, has touched, if not changed, me. I am indebted to all of you.

Feedback and Answers

CHAPTER TWO

Activities for Practice

1. a. You may experience a variety of feelings while watching your child involved in certain activities throughout the day. For example, during playtime, you may observe your child and experience a sense of peace and joy when seeing your child enjoy him/herself. However, at another time you may experience sadness. For instance, you may observe your child at resttime and begin to think about all the ways hearing loss affects his or her life. Or, you may see your child with hearing children in the neighborhood and become angry about your child's hearing loss.

1. b. Whatever the feelings you experience when observing your child, make note of them. This will help you in becoming more aware of the feelings you experience and the reasons for these feelings.

2. Parents express many different reactions to the discovery of the hearing loss condition in their child. Most parents share that this experience involves a great deal of adjustment and strength to cope with the changes in their lives. Most notable of the parents' descriptions of this period is the wide range of feelings that the diagnosis creates. Writing your personal thoughts about this part of your life can bring forth some of the same feelings that you experienced at the time your child's hearing loss was diagnosed. It is important to recognize that these feelings exist and that it is all right to experience them. Reviewing this aspect of your life can demonstrate to you the ways you have handled this difficult situation. Some parents say that they developed inner strength from this period in their lives.

The diagnosis of hearing loss in your child and the implications of hearing loss on your child's life creates definite changes in your life and in your family. Writing the letter in this activity can give you the opportunity to reflect on how the hearing loss has affected you. One parent shared this message in her letter: "We are finally growing stronger day by day. My husband and I are trying to be as supportive as possible to each other. Sometimes we take turns being the strong one. At any rate we are doing fine. We still have our moments, but what family doesn't?"

3. Individuals handle difficult situations in different ways. The way you handle an uncomfortable situation or difficult feelings is the way you cope. You may cope with the feeling of sadness or depression by sleeping. Or you may handle this type of feeling by making yourself busy with other activities to avoid focusing on the discomfort. You may use different ways to deal with each of the feelings listed in this activity.

4. A social support group involves the people around you that you can depend on when needing support at a time of need. Social support has been shown to buffer against the effects of stress caused by emotional and physical problems. Your social support system is an excellent resource to help you cope and adjust to everyday problems.

5. It is important to determine which people in your personal social support group you can rely on during difficult times such as when you need to discuss your feelings and which people in the group you can only rely on under little or no stress, such as when you need to go to a movie or go out dancing to help you relieve some tension. Knowing the different ways you can depend on members in your personal social support group will give you the direction you need on how to use the group most effectively.

6. It is important not to ignore your child's comments and questions about hearing loss. You can offer an explanation in language and terms the child understands. You can explain to your child that "all people are different. And, that one way you are different is that you can't hear." You can also explain how your child became deaf or hard of hearing. If no explanation exists, your child should be told and reminded how special, unique, and important he or she is.

CHAPTER THREE

Activities for Practice

1. People cope with difficult feelings or situations in different ways. Reviewing the ten suggestions for coping with your feelings listed at the end of chapter three (pp. 27–28) may give you ideas of different ways to deal with your particular circumstances. The final suggestion listed offers a few specific ways people use to cope. As you begin to think about ways to handle strong feelings, you may discover a new strategy for coping that can help you. Talking to others can help you cope. Not only can speaking to someone about your feelings make you feel better, but you may discover additional ways of coping through another's suggestions.

2. Hearing loss may affect your life and your child's life in a variety of ways. For example, hearing loss will affect how your child communicates with you. It may frustrate you when you cannot understand what your child wants or needs. A way to handle this feeling of frustration is to attempt to calm down before trying to communicate further. You might go into an area in the home free from distractions in order to focus primarily on the child and his or her needs. Hearing loss does make your child different from you. Even with a hearing aid, your child may hear some sounds and not others. For instance, when listening to music you may feel sad because you cannot share this experience with your child. You can cope with this situation by involving the child in experiences that both of you can share. Or, you may need to discuss these sad feelings with someone else.

3. Many parents have shared that the discovery of hearing loss has greatly influenced their lives. For example, during the diagnosis period, parents experience many different feelings such as sadness, anger, frustration, and confusion. In experiencing these feelings, parents discover different ways to cope that can be useful in the future. Some share that the condition has brought the family closer, enabling them to rely on one another's strengths. This experience also helps some develop a better understanding about the plight of those who belong to minority groups, including individuals with different types of disabilities, certain ethnic groups, etc. Also, some par-

ents have shared that they have experienced a new culture by involving their family and friends with deaf and hard of hearing adults and interacting with others in the Deaf community.

4. and 5. If you do not know another parent with a deaf or hard of hearing child, you might need to contact your school district, a local audiology center, or other organizations to find out how to meet other parents. Parent groups may meet at these locations and you may be able to contact other parents through support groups. Sources for parents are located in chapter eleven. Some of the organizations listed may provide you with information concerning how to meet parents of deaf and hard of hearing children in your area. Additionally, contacting deaf and hard of hearing parents is especially critical in helping you in understanding hearing loss and in experiencing the Deaf community.

6. Many individuals report that writing in journals helps them to express their innermost thoughts and feelings. Writing in a journal not only helps you to express these thoughts and feelings, but also enables you to reflect on them at the moment or at another time. Some people find it easier to write thoughts and feelings down on paper, rather than to share them with another.

7. Activities related to understanding and expressing feelings encourage all family members to express themselves in a safe environment. Teaching your child at an early age to talk about his or her feelings will teach coping strategies for the future. It is important to note that helping children to label and understand feelings is a complicated process that should start early in a child's life. Feeling words are abstract and often difficult for children to understand.

8. It is important to express how you feel about this situation. If feelings or emotions are strong, it would be wise to calm down before acting. One response may be to check your child's reaction to see if he or she can handle the situation on his or her own. It may be necessary to explain to your child that some people do not understand about being deaf or hard of hearing, and they may act foolishly because of their lack of understanding. If you are concerned about your child's immediate reaction, you might guide your child from the situation to another activity.

CHAPTER FOUR

Activities for Practice

1. Nonverbal behaviors add meaning to the verbal message. It is difficult to imagine our communications with others without the use of facial expressions, gestures, and body language.

2. Individuals use various nonverbal behaviors to convey their messages. Just as different people use different nonverbal behaviors to convey messages, different people may read nonverbal communications differently. You can try this exercise to illustrate this point. Try to demonstrate these feelings to another person using only facial expressions: hostility, concern, and boredom. Check to see if the other person can select which feeling you are attempting to convey. This activity, similar to that of Activity 1, will help demonstrate the power of nonverbal behaviors in conveying messages. Being aware of nonverbal behaviors will help you recognize the importance of these messages to your child. Being aware of nonverbal behaviors and their impact on communication will also help you read your deaf or hard of hearing child's nonverbal cues.

3. This activity helps you be more aware of the use and the importance of nonverbal language in our communication system. You can discover a great deal of information about others through their use of nonverbal behaviors. Picking up on these behaviors, however, is not easy. We are used to communicating verbally. We are not as practiced in using our vision to determine a message. Deaf and hard of hearing individuals, including your child, are very skilled at using their visual abilities. We need to develop the capability of using and interpreting nonverbal behavior like any other skill. Practice is important. Practice exercises will help you become more aware of nonverbal communication and its use.

4. Your child will rely on nonverbal communication much more than his or her hearing peers. It is therefore important to actively practice techniques to enhance your skills in nonverbal communication. For example, getting down to your child's eye level to communicate will help him or her see your facial expressions and eyes, which provide vital information concerning your messages. When using the techniques suggested in chapter four, observe if your child responds better during your

interactions. Continue to use these techniques and practice these methods consistently when you interact with your child.

5. Mary's mother's nonverbal behavior is inconsistent with the message she wants to communicate. Also, the mother's business associates are reinforcing Mary's behavior by saying, "Isn't she sweet!" Finally, attention is reinforcing Mary's behavior.

CHAPTER FIVE

Activities for Practice

1. a. Dinnertime conversations have been found to be an important link to increased language development in children. You can begin with small amounts of sharing around the table. Be sure that all family members pay attention to one another while communicating.

1. b. A "communication spoon" has been used by some families to monitor the flow of conversation so all members can follow the interactions. Some families have used a "koosh" or soft, small ball that they toss to the person who wants to communicate. Of course, the ball would not be a good idea to use at the dinner table, but it could be used to monitor the communication flow during a family meeting.

2. Family meetings have been suggested by many professionals who work with families. These professionals believe that all families should practice this activity faithfully to prevent family conflicts and to encourage family unity.

3. A family scrapbook not only makes each member feel important to the family structure but also helps your deaf or hard of hearing child feel a sense of belonging to the family unit through an activity that involves his or her channel of communication—visual aspects of language. Using this visual device, a discussion can result about family history. Also, the scrapbook can encourage language development since family stories are detailed by all family members.

4. Telling and acting out stories are important features of the Deaf community and culture. Your child can actually be involved in this activity with or without picture prompts. In other words, your child can act out or mime various features of a

story. Games like Pictionary could be an excellent tool that combines storytelling with the use of visual material. Be creative with developing your story ideas.

5. Remember that your child's environment is a visual one. You need to think about the effects divided attention has on his or her world and practice communication while being aware of your child's visual needs.

6. See #4. Additionally, storytime or storytelling helps develop a child's language base. You can practice your nonverbal and/or visual language abilities by acting out the stories. Storytelling not only increases language skills but it also teaches a child how to pay attention to important details in a story and how to take turns. It provides an intimate time to share yourself with your child—a special time to be together.

And finally, if reading a story is part of the bedtime routine for your child, it helps him or her know what to expect each evening. Many parents report that getting their child to go to bed is a difficult chore. They have found that using storytime after the child's bath and before going to bed helps set the child's expectations for bedtime and sleep.

7. Evaluating your family's communication system in your home on an ongoing basis is critical. Since communication is the primary vehicle to express and share ideas in all families, it is often the primary obstacle to stable family life in hearing families with deaf or hard of hearing children. Evaluating your communication system in your home will help you to be aware of all of your family members' needs in a consistent manner.

CHAPTER SIX

Activities for Practice

1. a. Be very specific about the behaviors you observe; for example, Sam was very calm, he came home and wanted to rest in his room; Sue was extremely noisy—she threw and slammed her books on the table, slammed doors, yelled and screamed at her brothers and sisters; Charlie completed all of his homework, he was able to work for thirty minutes without a break.

1. b. It is important for you to consider whether the behaviors in your child are age appropriate or inappropriate. Use what you believe to be typical behavior at a particular age to judge if the behavior is appropriate.

Examples:

Three-year-old hard of hearing child:

Behavior	Age-appropriate	Age-inappropriate
Hitting others to get their attention.	Not unusual behavior for a child of this age.	

Ten-year-old deaf child:

Behavior	Age-appropriate	Age-inappropriate
Hitting others to get their attention.		Age inappropriate, unusual behavior for a child this age.

1. c. As a parent of a deaf or hard of hearing child, you must view your child's behavior in light of what is considered "normal" for all children. This will be helpful for several reasons. First, it can help you understand what is generally expected of a youngster your child's age. Second, you can compare the differences between what is expected and what behavior you observe. This can help you decide if the behavior is appropriate or inappropriate. Third, and most important, understanding what is expected gives you a starting point for determining what impact hearing loss has on your child. Even if you believe the behavior to be inappropriate, you may have a better understanding of why the behavior occurs. Developing an understanding can help you determine the best course of action to take.

2. When you are deciding on whether your child's behavior is age-appropriate or age-inappropriate, note whether the behavior is part of an ongoing pattern or if it just recently developed. If the behavior has been occurring over a long period of time, it may be a habit or a part of your child's personality. If it is a new behavior, it could be a reaction to changes in your child's emotional, social, or physical growth. For example, a child reaching puberty may exhibit a variety of behaviors not seen

before—irritability, mood swings, acting-out behavior; a child attending school for the first time may display behaviors such as crying or acting fearful or withdrawn. These new behaviors reflect the changes in your child's life. Being aware that life changes can affect behavior can help you understand the behavior and judge whether it is appropriate or inappropriate.

3. A tantrum is not age-appropriate for this child. This parent needs to set clear limits on the child's inappropriate behavior. However, this behavior may be related to problems in communication.

CHAPTER SEVEN

Activities for Practice

1. Playtime: Rule—Put your toys away when finished playing.

2. Parents can use a variety of ways to convey limits. It may be helpful to show or demonstrate the limit to your child. For example, while your child is sitting at the dinner table, you can show him or her appropriate behavior. You can also demonstrate unacceptable behaviors, following this with another demonstration of what is expected. Some parents find it helpful to devise a picture book to illustrate the limits (e.g., a toy box drawn with toys scattered on the floor around it, arrows drawn from the toys pointing toward the toy box). The pictures contained in the picture book serve as visual reminders of rules and limits.

   Using Polaroid pictures of your child practicing the appropriate behaviors for each rule has been a favorite technique of parents, teachers, and children alike. Your child will love being included in the photographs and will remember the rules better since he or she is an integral part of them. You can place these photographs next to the corresponding rule.

3. You need to follow through on the rules and limits consistently. If you are not consistent in giving the consequences you have decided upon, your child can become confused and believe the limits are not important. All children will occasionally test limits. You must place consequences on your child's behavior when the limit is followed (reward or reinforcement) and when it is not followed (punishment, ignoring, etc.).

4. You need to set limits on your child's behavior. For example, you may decide that the chores must be done before your child can receive some reward. Your limits should be stated in positive, clear terms and followed up on consistently. Example of limit: All chores must be completed before leaving the house.

CHAPTER EIGHT

Activities for Practice

1. Parents differ in what they believe to be misbehavior in children. One parent may perceive his or her child making loud noises as misbehavior, and another may not find this behavior troublesome. On the other hand, many parents may consider refusal to do what a child is told to be defiant and inappropriate behavior. Only you can define what you believe to be misbehavior in your child. You must also examine the response you give your child when he or she misbehaves. Your response will generally determine whether your child's behavior will continue. For example, if your child consistently does not do the chores you request around the home, you can ignore the child's behavior or act on it by acknowledging the misbehavior and providing an appropriate consequence (such as taking away certain privileges). Although there is no one right way to respond to your child's misbehavior, you can determine if your response was effective by examining whether the behavior changes as a result of the consequence.

2. This activity helps parents to look more closely at their interactions with their children. It is helpful to recall as much of the interaction involving the misbehavior as possible. It may be worthwhile to do several A-B-C patterns involving situations where the behavior occurs only occasionally. You may then see the types of responses or consequences that encourage the child to continue the behavior. For example, if a child seems to fight with other children or argue with peers, you might apply the A-B-C pattern on several occasions when this behavior occurs. You may discover some similarities in each of the situations that is encouraging your child's behavior to occur. In completing the A-B-C pattern over time, you may see that your youngster has trouble interacting with others when involved in games or structured activities. This type of situation requires the child

to follow rules. Perhaps the antecedent event is that the child docs not know the rules or how to follow the rules consistently, and this has led to the child's difficulty in interacting with his or her peers. Or, perhaps the child is getting attention due to problematic behavior during these activities.

3.

A Antecedents	B Behavior	C Consequences
Sam's demanding occurs in and out of the house, but is more intense in public. Demanding seldom occurs with father. Demanding occurs when mother doesn't respond to his requests.	Sam demands that his mother give or buy him things. When mother does not respond, Sam gets angry and shouts and screams.	Mother interacts with Sam a lot when the demanding occurs. She pleads and begs Sam to stop. Sometimes she gets tired and gives in.

4.

A Antecedents	B Behavior	C Consequences
Johnny doesn't like homework. Teacher has not received homework. Television in room. Papers torn up.	Watching TV. Not doing homework.	Watching TV is fun. Getting out of homework.

Recognizing this pattern is helpful in understanding what encourages the child's behavior. Antecedents and consequences contribute to misbehavior. For example, a television in the room where the child is supposed to be doing homework entices the child (antecedent). The child receives pleasurable outcomes—enjoys TV, relaxes without doing homework—for the behavior (consequences).

Deafness-Related Resources for Parents

EDUCATIONAL PLACEMENT AND INFORMATION

Alexander Graham Bell Association for the Deaf
3417 Volta Place, NW
Washington, DC 20007
(202) 337-5220

American Organization for the Education of the Hearing-Impaired
3417 Volta Place, NW
Washington, DC 20007
(202) 337-5220

Coalition for Equal Education of Deaf Students
5569 Gloucester Street
Churchton, MD 20733

Clearinghouse on Disabilities
Office of Special Education and Rehabilitative Services
300 C Street SW, Room 3132
Washington, DC 20202
(202) 205-8241 (Voice/TTY)

Close Up Foundation
1235 Jefferson Davis Highway
Arlington, VA 22202
(703) 892-5400 (Voice)
(703) 892-5143 (TTY)

The Conference of Educational Administrators Serving the Deaf
Lexington School for the Deaf
75th Street and 30th Avenue
Jackson Heights, NY 11370
(718) 899-8800 (Voice)
(718) 899-3030 (TTY)

The Convention of American Instructors of the Deaf
P.O. Box 377
Bedford, TX 76095
(817) 354-8414 (Voice/TTY)

The Council for Exceptional Children
1920 Association Drive
Reston, VA 22091
(703) 620-3660 (Voice/TTY)

Council on Education of the Deaf (CED)
Box 68
Ida, MI 48140
(313) 269-3875

The National Clearinghouse for Bilingual Education (NCBE)
1118 22nd Street, NW
Washington, DC 20037
(202) 467-0867
1-800-321-NCBE

The National Committee for Citizens in Education
10840 Little Patuxent Parkway, Suite 301
Columbia, MD 21044

National Information Center for
Children and Youth with Disabilities
P.O. Box 1492
Washington, DC 20013
(800) 695-0285 (Voice/TTY)

National Information Center on Deafness
Gallaudet University
800 Florida Avenue NE
Washington, DC 20002
(202) 651-5051 (Voice)
(202) 651-5052 (TTY)

Special Office for Materials Distribution
Indiana University Audio-Visual Center
Bloomington, IN 47401
This center distributes educational captioned films and other
teaching aids for deaf and hard of hearing people.

TRIPOD
2901 N. Keystone Street
Burbank, CA 91504

(818) 972-2080 (Voice/TTY)
(800) 972-2080

United States Department of Education
Captioning and Adaptation Branch
Division of Educational Services
Office of Special Education Programs
600 Independence Avenue SW
Washington, DC 20202
(202) 205-9172 (Voice)
(202) 205-8170 (TTY)

HEARING AIDS AND ASSISTIVE DEVICES

Alexander Graham Bell Association for the Deaf
3417 Volta Place, NW
Washington, DC 20007
(202) 337-5220 (Voice/TTY)

American Academy of Otolaryngology—Head and Neck Surgery
One Prince Street
Alexandria, VA 22314
(703) 836-4444 (Voice)
(703) 519-1585 (TTY)

American Hearing Research Foundation
55 E. Washington Street, Suite 2022
Chicago, IL 60602
(312) 726-9670 (Voice)

American Speech-Language-Hearing Association
10801 Rockville Pike
Rockville, MD 20852
(301) 897-5700 (Voice/TTY)
(800) 638-8255 (Voice/TTY)

AT&T National Special Needs Center
2001 Route 46
Parsippany, NJ 07054
(800) 273-1222 (Voice)
(800) 833-3232 (TTY)

Better Hearing Institute
5021B Backlick Road
Annandale, VA 22003
(703) 642-0580 (Voice/TTY)
(800) EAR-WELL

Com-Tek
375 West Lemel Circle
Salt Lake City, UT 84115
(415) 383-4000

The EAR Foundation
2000 Church Street, Box 111
Nashville, TN 37236
(615) 329-7807

Gallaudet University Audiology Department
800 Florida Avenue, NE
Washington, DC 20002
(202) 651-5329 (Voice/TTY)

Hal-Hen Co.
35-53 24th Street
Long Island, NY 11106
(718) 392-6020

Hear Now
4001 S. Magnolia Way
Suite 100
Denver, CO 80237
(800) 648-4327

House Ear Institute
2100 W. Third Street
5th Floor
Los Angeles, CA 90057
(213) 483-4431 (Voice)
(213) 484-2642 (TTY)
(800) 352-8888 (Voice /TTY); Parenting hotline

LS&S Group, Inc.
P.O. Box 673

Northbrook, IL 60065
(800) 468-4789 (Voice)
(800) 317-8533 (TTY)

National Association for Hearing and Speech Action
10801 Rockville Pike
Rockville, MD 20852
(800) 638-TALK

National Captioning Institute
1900 Gallows Road, Suite 3000
Vienna, VA 22182
(703) 917-7600 (Voice/TTY)
(800) 374-3986 (Voice/TTY)

National Flashing Signal Systems (NFSS)
8120 Fenton Street
Silver Spring, MD 20910
(301) 589-6671 (Voice)
(301) 589-6670 (TTY)

National Hearing Aid Society
20361 Middlebelt Road
Livonia, MI 48152
(313) 478-2610 (Voice/TTY)
(800) 521-5248; Hearing Aid Helpline

National Hearing Association
1010 Jorie Boulevard, #308
Oak Brook, IL 60521
(312) 323-7200

National Technical Institute for the Deaf
1 Lomb Memorial Drive
Rochester, NY 14623
(716) 475-2894 (Voice/TTY)

Phonic Ear Inc.
250 Camino Alto
Mill Valley, CA 94941
(415) 383-4000

Tele-Consumer Hotline
1910 K Street, NW, Suite 610
Washington, DC 20006
(202) 223-4371
(800) 332-1124

Telex Communications, Inc.
9600 Aldrich Avenue South
Minneapolis, MN 55420
(612) 884-7430

OCCUPATIONAL AND REHABILITATIVE SERVICES

Academy of Rehabilitative Audiology
Department of Psychology
University of Maryland, Baltimore City
5401 Wilkens Avenue
Baltimore, MD 21228
(301) 455-2364 (Voice)

American Deafness and Rehabilitation Association
P.O. Box 251554
Little Rock, AR 72225
(501) 868-8850 (Voice/TTY)

Deaf Counseling, Advocacy, and Referral Agency
22289 Pearce Street
Hayward, CA 94541
(510) 733-3850 (TTY)

Deafness and Communicative Disorders Branch
Rehabilitation Services Administration
Department of Education
330 C Street SW, Room 3228
Washington, DC 20202
(202) 205-9152 (Voice)
(202) 205-8352 (TTY)
(800) 735-2258

Helen Keller National Center for Deaf-Blind
Youth and Adults

111 Middle Neck Road
Sands Point, NY 11050
(516) 944-8900 (Voice)
(516) 944-8637 (TTY)

National Center on Employment of the Deaf
National Technical Institute for the Deaf
52 Lomb Memorial Drive
Rochester, NY 14623
(716) 475-6205 (Voice/TTY)

National Crisis Center for the Deaf
University of Virginia Medical Center
Box 48
Charlottesville, VA 22908
(800) 446-9876 (TTY)
Provides 24-hour TTY access to emergency services for deaf persons
in case of sudden illness, injury, poisoning, or fire.

National Healthcare Foundation for the Deaf
3722 12th Street NE
Washington, DC 20017
(202) 832-6681

National Rehabilitation Information Center
8455 Colesville Road, Suite 935
Silver Spring, MD 20910
(301) 588-9284 (Voice)
(301) 495-5626 (TTY)

Rehabilitation Services Administration
Deafness and Communicative Disorder Branch
Switzer Building, Room 3414
330 C Street, SW
Washington, DC 20202
(202) 732-1398 (Voice/TTY)

ORGANIZATIONS FOR DEAF PEOPLE

Advocates for Hearing-Impaired Youth
P.O. Box 75949
Washington, DC 20013
(301) 868-7593 (Voice/TTY; evenings and weekends)

Alexander Graham Bell Association for the Deaf
3417 Volta Place, NW
Washington, DC 20007
(202) 337-5220 (Voice/TTY)

American Association of the Deaf-Blind, Inc.
814 Thayer Avenue
Silver Spring, MD 20910
(301) 588-6545 (TTY)

American Athletic Association of the Deaf
3607 Washington Boulevard #4
Ogden, UT 84402
(801) 393-8710 (Voice)
(801) 393-7916 (TTY)

American Sign Language Teachers Association
814 Thayer Avenue
Silver Spring, MD 20910
(301) 587-1788 (TTY)

Captioned Films for the Deaf
Modern Talking Pictures Services, Inc.
5000 Park Street North
St. Petersburg, FL 33709
(800) 237-6213 (Voice/TTY)

Deafpride, Inc.
Chapel Hall
Gallaudet University
800 Florida Avenue NE
Washington, DC 20002
(202) 675-6700 (Voice/TTY)

Episcopal Conference of the Deaf
P.O. Box 27459
Philadelphia, PA 19118
(215) 247-1059 (Voice)
(215) 247-6454 (TTY)

Gallaudet University
800 Florida Avenue NE
Washington, DC 20002
(202) 651-5000 (Voice/TTY)

Greater Los Angeles Council on Deafness (GLAD), Inc.
2222 Laverna Avenue
Los Angeles, CA 90041
(213) 478-8000 (Voice/TTY)

International Lutheran Deaf Association
1333 S. Kirkwood Road
St. Louis, MO 63122
(314) 965-9917 (Voice/TTY)
(800) 433-3954 (Voice/TTY)

Junior National Association of the Deaf Youth Program
445 N. Pennsylvania Street, Suite 804
Indianapolis, IN 46204

National Association of the Deaf
814 Thayer Avenue
Silver Spring, MD 20910
(301) 587-1788 (Voice)
(301) 587-1789 (TTY)

National Catholic Office for the Deaf
7202 Buchanan Street
Landover Hills, MD 20784
(301) 577-1684 (Voice)
(301) 577-4184 (TTY)

National Congress of Jewish Deaf
9420 Reseda #442
Northridge, CA 91324
(818) 993-2517 (TTY)

National Fraternal Society of the Deaf
1300 W. Northwest Highway
Mt. Prospect, IL 60056
(847) 392-9282 (Voice)
(847) 392-1409 (TTY)

National Technical Institute for the Deaf
Rochester Institute of Technology
One Lomb Memorial Drive
Rochester, NY 14623
(716) 475-2894 (TTY)

National Theatre of the Deaf
5 West Main Street
Chester, CT 06412
(203) 526-4132 (TTY)

Organization for the Use of the Telephone, Inc.
P.O. Box 175
Owing Mills, MD 21117
(301) 655-1827 (Voice)

Registry of Interpreters for the Deaf, Inc. (RID)
8630 Fenton Street
Silver Spring, MD 20910
(301) 608-0500 (Voice)
(301) 608-0562 (TTY)

Self-Help for Hard of Hearing People, Inc. (SHHH)
7910 Woodmont Avenue, Suite 1200
Bethesda, MD 20814
(301) 657-2248 (Voice)
(301) 657-2249 (TTY)

Telecommunications for the Deaf, Inc.
8719 Colesville Road
Suite 300
Silver Spring, MD 20910
(301) 589-3786 (Voice)
(301) 589-3006 (TTY)

World Federation of the Deaf
Iilantie 4, P. O. Box 65
Helsinki, Finland 00401
358 0 58031 (Voice)

World Recreation Association of the Deaf, Inc.
1550 San Leandro Boulevard

Mail Slot #196
San Leandro, CA 94577
(510) 845-2328 (TTY)

PARENTING RESOURCES

American Society for Deaf Children
2848 Arden Way, Suite 210
Sacramento, CA 95825
(800) 942-2732 (Voice/TTY)

Council for Exceptional Children
1920 Association Drive
Reston, VA 22091
(703) 620-3660 (Voice/TTY)

John Tracy Clinic
806 West Adams Boulevard
Los Angeles, CA 90007
(213) 747-2924 (TTY)
(213) 748-5481 (Voice)
(800) 522-4582

National Cued Speech Association
1658 Oberlin Road
Raleigh, NC 27662
(919) 828-1218 (Voice/TTY)

Parent Educational Advocacy Training Center
228 S. Pitt Street, Suite 300
Alexandria, VA 22314
(703) 836-3026 (TTY)
(703) 836-2953 (Voice)

Parent to Parent
256 South Lake Street
Los Angeles, CA 90057
(213) 484-2642 TTY
(213) 483-4431 Voice

SEE Center for the Advancement of Deaf Children
P. O. Box 1181
Los Alamitos, CA 90720
(310) 430-1467 (TTY/Voice)

Self-Help for Hard of Hearing People, Inc. (SHHH)
7910 Woodmont Avenue
Suite 1200
Bethesda, MD 20814
(301) 657-2249 (TTY)
(301) 657-2248 (Voice)

PUBLICATIONS

The Broadcaster
The Deaf American
National Association of the Deaf
814 Thayer Avenue
Silver Spring, MD 20910

The Deafpride Advocate
Deafpride, Inc.
800 Florida Avenue NE
Washington, DC 20002

The Endeavor
American Society for Deaf Children
814 Thayer Avenue
Silver Spring, MD 20910

Junior NAD Newsletter
NAD Youth Program
445 N. Pennsylvania Street
Suite 804
Indianapolis, IN 46204

Perspectives in Education and Deafness
Pre-College National Missions Programs
Gallaudet University
Washington, DC 20002

Silent News
Silent News, Inc.
133 Gaither Drive, Suite E
Mt. Laurel, NJ 08054-1710

World Around You
Pre-College National Missions Programs
Gallaudet University
Washington, DC 20002

PUBLISHERS AND BOOKSTORES

Dawn Sign Press
6130 Nancy Ridge Drive
San Diego, CA 92121
(619) 625-0600 (Voice/TTY)

Deaf Counseling, Advocacy, and Referral
Agency (DCARA) Bookstore
157 Parrott Street
San Leandro, CA 94577
(510) 351-3938 (Voice/TTY)

Gallaudet University Bookstore
800 Florida Avenue NE
Washington, DC 20002
(202) 651-5271(Voice/TTY)

Gallaudet University Press
800 Florida Avenue NE
Washington, DC 20002-3695
(202) 651-5488 (Voice/TTY)

Greater Los Angeles Council on Deafness, Inc.,
Bookstore
616 South Westmoreland Avenue
Los Angeles, CA 90005
(213) 383-2220 (Voice/TTY)

Harris Communications
15159 Technology Drive

Eden Prairie, MN 55344-3248
(800) 825-6758 (Voice)
(800) 825-9187 (TTY)

Modern Signs Press
10443 Los Alamitos Blvd.
Los Alamitos, CA 90720
(310) 493-4168 (Voice/TTY)

National Association of the Deaf Bookstore
814 Thayer Avenue
Silver Spring, MD 20910
(301) 587-1788 (Voice/TTY)

Sign Media, Inc.
4020 Blackburn Lane
Burtonsville, MD 20866
(301) 421-4460 (Voice/TTY)

T.J. Publishers
817 Silver Spring Avenue, #206
Silver Spring, MD 20910
(301) 585-4440 (Voice/TTY)

Children's Reinforcement Survey Schedule

You can use this reinforcement schedule (adapted from Cautela and Meisles in Goldstein 1995, pp. 228–34) with your child or you can use it as a guide to specific reinforcers.

	Dislike	Like	Like Very Much
1. Do you like candy?			
2. Do you like raisins?			
3. Do you like milk?			
4. Do you like apples?			
5. Do you like cereal?			
6. Do you like fruit juice?			
7. Do you like fruit?			
8. Do you like pop?			
9. Do you like to cook?			
10. Do you like music?			
11. Do you like stories?			
12. Do you like to read?			
13. Do you like going to the library?			
14. Do you like fairy tales?			
15. Do you like science fiction?			
16. Do you like mysteries?			
17. Do you like to write?			
18. Do you like cartoons and comic books?			
19. Do you like to play computer games?			
20. Do you like math?			
21. Do you like to color?			
22. Do you like to paint?			
23. Do you like making things from clay?			
24. Do you like making things out of wood?			

	Dislike	Like	Like Very Much
25. Do you like to play with toy cars?			
26. Do you like to play with model cars, trains, or airplanes?			
27. Do you like to fix things that are broken?			
28. Do you like to collect things?			
29. Do you like to play outdoors?			
30. Do you like playing at the playground?			
31. Do you like playing on swings?			
32. Do you like riding a bike?			
33. Do you like playing with children younger than you?			
34. Do you like playing with children older than you?			
35. Do you like taking care of a pet?			
36. Do you like playing with dogs?			
37. Do you like playing with cats?			
38. Do you like to ride in a car?			
39. Do you like watching trucks, bulldozers, and tractors?			
40. Do you like going on field trips?			
41. Do you like going to the mall?			
42. Do you like going to a restaurant?			
43. Do you like going to a circus or to a fair?			
44. Do you like to go to the zoo?			
45. Do you like to go on vacation?			
46. Do you like camping?			
47. Do you like to play board games?			
48. Do you like to watch television?			
49. Do you like to watch movies?			
50. Do you like to go to parties?			
51. Do you like swimming?			

	Dislike	Like	Like Very Much

52. Do you like roller skating?

53. Do you like ice skating?

54. Do you like hiking?

55. Do you like kickball?

56. Do you like soccer?

57. Do you like baseball?

58. Do you like football?

59. Do you like basketball?

60. Do you like hockey?

61. Do you like stuffed animals?

62. Do you like people to say, "You did a good job"?

63. Do you like being alone rather than with other people?

64. Do you like to be with a special grown-up?

65. What is your favorite thing to do?

_____

_____

_____

66. What makes you the most happy?

_____

_____

_____

Checklist for Evaluating Educational Programs

When the time comes for you to explore new programs for your child, it will help to take along a list of questions. In asking these questions, the age and school placement level of your child is of little concern. It is more important for you to secure a total picture of the educational program within a given school program or district. Through this list of questions, you can gain a sense of short- or long-range goals that a program has established to facilitate the learning process in deaf children.

Depending on the school program, your background and philosophy, and your child's needs, you may choose to emphasize some questions over others, or you may modify the questions to suit your own purposes. Regardless of your own experiences, the following questions may help you gather information to understand the basic qualities a program should have to provide a conducive learning environment for your child. Before making an informed choice about your child's educational program, it is important that you visit the program for an in-depth review of the areas presented below:

INSTRUCTIONAL PROGRAM/CURRICULUM

1. What is the philosophy of the school in relation to its educational curriculum?

2. What subject areas are covered daily in the child's educational program?

3. What curriculum is utilized in the various subject areas such as reading, science, math, sign and English languages, auditory training, etc.?

4. Are curriculum activities in each subject area age-appropriate for the children and do they follow state curriculum guidelines?

Note: These questions are adapted from a list prepared by Carl Kirchner at Tripod, Inc., and from a list of questions from the SEE Center for the Advancement of Deaf Children. (Please see appendix 1 for the addresses of these two organizations.)

5. What is the school's communication policy? Is it a written policy? (If yes, obtain a copy).

6. Specifically, what curriculum is followed in developing the child's overall language skills and the child's English language skills?

7. What sign system is used in the classroom by the teachers and requested for use at home by the parents?

8. Are speech, lipreading, and auditory training integrated as part of the content curriculum activities during the class day or are they a pull-out (separate) program?

9. If a sign system is used, are sign language classes available for interested hearing classmates?

10. Does the English language development program include extensive writing?

11. Does the classroom have a teacher aide?

12. Is appropriate homework given daily for the child?

13. What are some of the unique features of the entire program?

14. What kinds of opportunities for social skills development exist within the classroom?

15. How are the child's emotional (affective development) and psychological needs met in the classroom?

PHILOSOPHY AND ATTITUDES

16. What is the program's view on educating deaf and hard of hearing children? Is it a clinical, medical approach or one that comes from an educational or cultural point of view?

17. What can I expect the school to do for my child? What does the school expect me to do?

18. What are the expectations of the faculty and staff regarding deaf and hard of hearing children's capabilities?

19. What is the attitude on the part of the administrators, support staff, and teachers in regard to the Deaf community and Deaf culture?

20. What is the involvement of the faculty and staff within the Deaf community? For example, do they have deaf family members and/or friends?

21. What is the program's approach to discipline?

22. What kinds of resources are available to the children in relation to experiences that support interactions with other deaf children and adults, mainstreaming opportunities, field trip opportunities, etc.?

23. If mainstreaming opportunities are available, what kind of orientation is done for the deaf child and the receiving teacher before the child is placed in the mainstreamed class?

24. What is the school's philosophy on mainstreaming deaf children?

EVALUATION

25. What kind of assessment procedures are used with the child to identify cognitive abilities and academic strengths and need areas?

26. Is there an assessment system in place schoolwide?

27. What is the grading system? How is progress reported to parents?

ADMINISTRATIVE STRUCTURE AND ORGANIZATION

28. What is the structure of the program? Is it a day program, day class, regional program, or residential program, etc.?

29. Is there an administrator in charge of the deaf education program? If not, is there a supervising teacher or coordinator of the deaf education program who makes weekly visits to identify strengths and need areas within the educational programs for deaf children?

30. What is the basic funding source for this program?

31. What does the program offer in relation to extracurricular activities so that deaf and hearing children can interact with one another?

32. What does the high school program offer in terms of academic, vocational studies, and work experience activities?

33. What is the class composition? What is the age range? How many deaf children are in the program?

34. Is there a mixture of deaf and hard of hearing children in the class?

35. Are there any deaf and hard of hearing teachers and support staff such as teacher aides, counselors, social workers, psychologists, nurses, and secretaries, so that the children have deaf and hard of hearing role models?

36. Who is the person ultimately responsible for the program? What is her or his address and phone number?

37. Who is the on-site person responsible for the program? What is her or his address and phone number?

38. Is the transportation timetable reasonable?

FACULTY/STAFF QUALIFICATIONS

39. What are the competencies of the teachers in relation to sign language, speech, English language, and auditory skills development?

40. Are the receptive skills for ASL or for a manual code for English language sufficient on the part of the faculty, staff, and administrators? Do they really understand what the children are saying?

41. Is the faculty certified? Do they have state certification? CED certification? Advanced degrees?

SUPPORT SERVICES

42. What support service personnel are available to support the classroom teachers? Are there counselors, social workers, psychologists, interpreters, audiologists, speech and language specialists, reading specialists, ASL/Deaf Studies specialists, etc.?

43. What interpreting services are available? Are the interpreters nationally certified?

44. What notetaking services are available?

45. Are hearing aids worn consistently throughout the educational program?

46. What kinds of services are available to assist families in maintaining the hearing aid batteries, repairs, etc.?

47. What kind of amplification system is used in the classroom?

48. If a deaf child has another condition or is multihandicapped, how does the school handle services to meet his or her needs? What kinds of services are provided?

49. What resources are available for staff, students, and parents to learn about recent technology or methods used in educating deaf children? Is there a resource facility? Is there a media center? Are there resources for drama activities such as a stage and production equipment?

EXTRACURRICULAR ACTIVITIES

50. Are supervisors, administrators, faculty, and staff involved in after-school activities with the children?

51. What kinds of extracurricular activities are available for the students?

PARENT INVOLVEMENT

52. What additional support services are there for parents? Is there a support group to which any parent can belong?

53. Are there deaf parents that can be contacted who act as resources for other parents?

54. Are there parent education classes available to all parents?

55. Are sign language classes conveniently offered to parents?

56. How is the parent involved in the IEP process? Are parents actively involved in discussions about their child's needs?

57. Are parents welcome to make periodic observations in their child's classroom, as well as in other classrooms?

58. What is the communication network between home and school? Is it done by written messages; if so, daily or weekly? Who contacts the home and under what circumstances?

59. Are the child's files kept in the program's office? Can I have ready access to them as a parent? Who else will have access to my child's file?

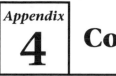

Comment Sheet

Name: _____

Address: _____

_____

_____

_____

_____

____ Parent   ____ Professional (specify) _____

Are you using this book   ____ with professional supervision?
____ without professional supervision?
____ other (specify) _____

Comments:

_____

_____

_____

_____

_____

_____

_____

_____

_____

Return to: Dr. John W. Adams
St. Mary's School for the Deaf
Psychological Services
2253 Main Street
Buffalo, NY 14214

Suggested Reading

COMMUNICATION CHOICES

American Annals of the Deaf. Washington, D.C.: Gallaudet University.

Andrews, J., and N. Taylor. 1987. From sign to print: A case study of picture book "reading" between mother and child. *Sign Language Studies* 56: 261–74.

Andrews, J., P. Winograud, and G. DeVille. 1996. Using sign language summaries during pre-reading lessons. *Teaching Exceptional Children* 28(3): 30–34.

Bonvillian, J. D., and R. J. Folven. 1990. The onset of signing in young children. In *SLR '87: Papers from the fourth international symposium on sign language research*, ed. W. Edmondson and F. Karlsson, 183–89. Hamburg, Germany: Signum Verlag.

Bornstein, H., K. Saulnier, and L. Hamilton. 1983. *The comprehensive Signed English dictionary*. Washington, D.C.: Gallaudet University Press.

Caccamise, F., and A. Drury. 1976. A review of current terminology in the education of the deaf. *The Deaf American* 29: 7–10.

Carbin, C. F. 1976. A total communication approach: A new program for deaf infants and children and their families. *British Columbia Medical Journal* 18.

Daniels, M. 1993. ASL as a factor in acquiring English. *Sign Language Studies* 78: 23–29.

Goldin-Meadow, S., and H. Feldman. 1975. The creation of a communication system: A study of deaf children of hearing parents. *Sign Language Studies* 8: 221–36.

Henegar, M. E. 1971. *Cued speech handbook for parents*. Washington, D.C.: Gallaudet College, Cued Speech Program.

Johnson, R. E., S. K. Liddell, and C. J. Erting. 1989. *Unlocking the curriculum: Principles for achieving access in Deaf education*. Gallaudet Research Institute Working Paper 89-3. Washington, D.C.: Gallaudet Research Institute.

Lawrence, E. D. 1979. *Sign language made simple*. Springfield, Mo.: Gospel Publishing House.

Ling, D., ed. 1984. *Early intervention for hearing-impaired children: Oral options*. Boston: College Hill Press.

————. 1984. *Early intervention for hearing-impaired children: Total communication options*. San Diego: College Hill Press.

Mahshie, S. N. 1994. A look at "sim-com" through new eyes. Paper presented at Especially for Parents: Everything You Always Wanted To Know About Bilingual/Bicultural Education But Were Afraid To Ask, 26 October, at Gallaudet University, Washington, D.C.

Meier, R. P., and E. L. Newport. 1990. Out of the hands of babes: On a possible sign advantage in language acquisition. *Language* 66: 1–23.

O'Neill, J., and H. Oyer. 1981. *Visual communication for the hard of hearing: History, research, methods*. 2d ed. Englewood Cliffs, N.J.: Prentice-Hall.

Pahz, J. A. 1978. *Total communication: The meaning behind the movement to expand educational opportunities for deaf children*. Springfield, Ill.: Charles C. Thomas.

Prier, O., B. Charlier, C. Hage, and J. Alegria. 1987. Evaluation of the effects of prolonged Cued Speech practice upon the reception of spoken language. In *The education of the Deaf: Current perspectives*, ed. I. G. Taylor, 616–28. New York: Croom Helm.

Royal National Institute for the Deaf. 1976. Methods of communication currently used in the education of the deaf. Paper read at residential seminar, 11–14 April 1975, at Roehampton, London, England.

Schwartz, S. 1996. *Choices in deafness: A parents' guide*. 2d ed. Bethesda, Md.: Woodbine House.

Spradley, T. S., and J. P. Spradley. 1985. *Deaf like me*. Washington, D.C.: Gallaudet University Press.

Strong, M. 1988. A bilingual approach to the education of young deaf children: ASL and English. In *Language learning and deafness*, ed. M. Strong, 113–29. Cambridge, England: Cambridge University Press.

Strong, M., and E. Charlson. 1988. Simultaneous communication: How teachers approach an impossible task. *American Annals of the Deaf* 132: 376–82.

The Volta Review. Washington, D.C.: Alexander Graham Bell Association for the Deaf.

Wilbur, R. 1991. *American Sign Language: Linguistic and applied dimensions*. Austin, Tex.: PRO-ED.

Williams-Scott, B., and E. Kipila. 1987. Cued speech: A professional point of view. In *Choices in Deafness: A parents' guide*, ed. S. Schwartz. Kensington, Md.: Woodbine House.

Winefield, R. 1987. *Never the twain shall meet: Bell, Gallaudet and the communications debate*. Washington, D.C.: Gallaudet University Press.

COPING WITH FEELINGS

Bernier, J. C. 1990. Parental adjustment to a disabled child: A family-systems perspective. *Families in Society: The Journal of Contemporary Human Services* 589–96.

Bowe, F., and M. Sternberg. 1973. *I'm deaf too—Twelve deaf Americans*. Silver Spring, Md.: National Association of the Deaf.

Cain, B. 1990. *Double-dip feelings: Stories to help children understand emotions*. (Gr. K–3). New York: Magination Press.

Crary, E. 1980. *One dozen feeling games*. (Gr. Pre–2). Seattle: Parenting Press.

Englemann, J. 1991. *Wonder what I feel today?: A coloring book about feelings*. (Gr. Pre–3). San Francisco: Hazeldon.

Featherstone, H. 1981. *A difference in the family: Living with a disabled child*. New York: Penguin Books.

Ferris, C. 1980. *A hug just isn't enough*. Washington, D.C.: Gallaudet University Press.

Fraser, G. R. 1976. *The causes of profound deafness in childhood: A study of 3,535 individuals with severe hearing losses present at birth or of childhood onset*. Baltimore, Md.: Johns Hopkins University Press.

Frederickson, J. 1985. *Life after deaf*. Silver Spring, Md.: National Association of the Deaf.

Glick, F. P., and D. R. Pellman. 1982. *Breaking silence: A family grows with deafness*. Scottsdale, Pa.: Herald Press.

Griffin, B. F., ed. 1980. *Family to family*. Washington, D.C.: Alexander Graham Bell Association for the Deaf.

Harvey, M. 1992. Dear mom and dad: If you only had known. *SHHH Journal* (September/October) 4–9.

Holland, R. 1988. *About me*. (Gr. K–5). Mt. Dora, Fla.: Kidsrights.

Koester L., and K. Meadow-Orlans. 1990. Parenting a deaf child: Stress, strength, and support. In *Educational and developmental aspects of deafness*, ed. D. Moores and K. Meadow-Orlans, 299–320. Washington, D.C.: Gallaudet University Press.

Love, H.D. 1970. *Parental attitudes toward exceptional children.* Springfield, Ill.: Charles C. Thomas.

Luterman, D. 1987. *Deafness in the family.* Boston: Little, Brown.

Neuman, S., and R. Panoff. 1983. *Exploring feelings: Activities for young children.* Encino, Calif.: Humanics.

Murphy, A.T. 1979. The families of handicapped children: Context for disability. *The Volta Review* 5: 265–78.

Naiman, D.W., and J.D. Schein. 1978. *For parents of deaf children.* Silver Spring, Md.: National Association of the Deaf.

Richards, J. 1982. *Dealing with feelings: A creative format for self-expression.* (Gr. 2–6). Santa Barbara, Calif.: Learning Works.

Ryan, E. 1992. A deaf child in the family: New reasons to hope? *Perspectives* 11: 14–17.

Schlesinger, H., and K.P. Meadow. 1976. Emotional support for parents. In *Teaching parents to teach: A guide to working with the special child*, ed. D.L. Lillie, P.L. Trohanis, and K.W. Goin, 35–47. New York: Walker.

Segal, M., and D. Adcock. 1987. *Feelings.* Encino, Calif.: Humanics.

Seligman, M. 1991. *The family with a handicapped child: Understanding and treatment.* 2d ed. Boston: Allyn & Bacon.

———. 1991. Grandparents of disabled grandchildren: Hopes, fears, and adaptation. *Families in Society: The Journal of Contemporary Human Services* 73(3): 147–52.

CULTURE

Baker, C., and R. Battison, eds. 1980. *Sign language and the Deaf community: Essays in honor of William C. Stokoe.* Silver Spring, Md.: National Association of the Deaf.

Batson, T. W., and E. Bergman, eds. 1985. *Angels and Outcasts: An anthology of deaf characters in literature*. Washington, D.C.: Gallaudet University Press.

Benderly, B. L. 1989. *Dancing without music: Deafness in America*. Washington, D.C.: Gallaudet University Press.

Bradford, T. 1991. *Say that again, please: Insights in dealing with hearing loss*. Austin, Tex.: T. H. Bradford.

Cagle, K., and S. Cagle. 1990. *GA to SK etiquette*. Bowling Green, Ohio: Bowling Green Press.

Cohen, L. H. 1994. *Train go, sorry: Inside a Deaf world*. Boston: Houghton Mifflin.

The Deaf American. Silver Spring, Md.: National Association of the Deaf.

Erting, C. J., R. C. Johnson, D. L. Smith, and B. D. Snider, eds. 1994. *The Deaf way: Perspectives from the international conference on deaf culture*. Washington, D.C.: Gallaudet University Press.

Gannon, J. R. 1981. *Deaf heritage: A narrative history of Deaf America*. Silver Spring, Md.: National Association of the Deaf.

Garretson, M. 1992. *Viewpoints on deafness*. Silver Spring, Md.: National Association of the Deaf.

Grant, B., ed. 1987. *The quiet ear: Deafness in literature*. London: Deutsch.

Hafer, J. C., and E. Ditman-Richmond. 1988. What hearing parents should know about deaf culture. *Perspectives for Teachers of the Hearing Impaired* (September/October): 2–5.

Heppner, C. M. 1992. *Seeds of disquiet: One deaf woman's experience*. Washington, D.C.: Gallaudet University Press.

Higgins, P. 1980. *Outsiders in a hearing world: A sociology of deafness*. New York: Sage Publications.

Holcomb, R. K. 1986. *Hazards of deafness*. Acton, Calif.: Joyce Media Publications.

Holcomb, R. K., S. Holcomb, and T. Holcomb. 1995. *Deaf culture, our way*. San Diego: Dawn Sign Press.

Jacobs, L. M. 1989. *A deaf adult speaks out*. 3d ed. Washington, D.C.: Gallaudet University Press.

Lane, H. 1989. *When the mind hears: A history of the Deaf*. New York: Vintage Books.

———. 1992. *The mask of benevolence: Disabling the Deaf community*. New York: Alfred A. Knopf.

Lane, L. G., and I. B. Pittle, eds. 1981. *A handful of stories*. Washington, D.C.: Gallaudet College, Division of Public Services.

Meadow, K. P. 1977. Name signs as identity symbols in the deaf community. *Sign Language Studies* 16: 237–46.

Moore, M. S., and L. Levitan. 1993. *For hearing people only: Answers to some of the most commonly asked questions about the Deaf community, its culture and the "Deaf" reality*. 2d ed. Rochester, N.Y.: Deaf Life Press.

Neisser, A. 1990. *The other side of silence: Sign language and the Deaf community in America*. Washington, D.C.: Gallaudet University Press.

Padden, C., and T. Humphries. 1988. *Deaf in America: Voices from a culture*. Cambridge: Harvard University Press.

Panara, R., and J. Panara. 1983. *Great deaf Americans*. Silver Spring, Md.: T. J. Publishers.

Robinette, D. C. 1990. *Hometown heroes*. Washington, D.C.: Gallaudet University Press.

Rosen, R. 1986. Deafness: A social perspective. In *Deafness in perspective*, ed. D. Luterman, 241–61. San Diego: College Hill Press.

Rutherford, S. 1987. *A study of American Deaf folklore*. Burtonsville, Md.: Linstok Press.

Sacks, O. 1989. *Seeing voices: A journey into the world of the Deaf*. Berkeley: University of California Press.

Schein, J. D. 1989. *At home among strangers: Exploring the Deaf community in the United States*. Washington, D.C.: Gallaudet University Press.

Toole, D. K. 1981. *Successful deaf Americans*. Beaverton, Ore.: Dormac.

Treesberg, J. 1988. Let the Deaf be Deaf: A hearing mother in the Deaf revolution. *Washington Post*, 5 April.

Van Cleve, J. V., ed. 1986. *Gallaudet encyclopedia of Deaf people and deafness*. New York: McGraw-Hill.

———. 1993. *Deaf history unveiled: Interpretations from the new scholarship*. Washington, D.C.: Gallaudet University Press.

Wilcox, S., ed. 1989. *American Deaf culture: An anthology*. Burtonsville, Md.: Linstok Press.

Wilcox, S., and P. P. Wilcox. 1996. *Learning to see: Teaching American Sign Language as a second language*. Washington, D.C.: Gallaudet University Press.

EDUCATIONAL PLACEMENT

Bernstein, M. E., and J. Martin. 1992. Informing parents about educational options: How well are we doing? *American Annals of the Deaf* 137: 31–39.

Brill, R. G. 1978. *Mainstreaming the prelingually deaf child: A study of the status of prelingually deaf children in various patterns of mainstreamed education for hearing impaired children*. Washington, D.C.: Gallaudet College Press.

Craig, H. B. 1992. Parent-infant education in schools for deaf children before and after PL 99–457. *American Annals of the Deaf* 137: 69–78.

The Deaf American. Silver Spring, Md.: National Association of the Deaf.

The Endeavor. Silver Spring, Md.: American Society for Deaf Children.

Garretson, M. D. 1977. The residential school. *The Deaf American* 29: 19–22.

Goppold, L. 1988. Early intervention for preschool deaf children: The longitudinal academic effects related to program methodology. *American Annals of the Deaf* 133: 285–88.

Katz, L., S. Mathis, and E. C. Merrill. 1978. *The deaf child in the public schools: A handbook for parents*. Danville, Ill.: Interstate Printers and Publishers.

Madden, N. A., and R. E. Slavin. 1983. Mainstreaming students with mild handicaps: Academic and social outcomes. *Review of Educational Research* 53: 519–69.

McAfee, J. K., and G. A. Vekgason. 1979. Parent involvement in the process of special education: Establishing a new partnership. *Focus on Exceptional Children* 2: 1–13.

The NAD Broadcaster. Silver Spring, Md.: National Association of the Deaf.

Nix, G. W. 1977. The rights of hearing-impaired children. *The Volta Review* 79 (Monograph).

Opton, K. 1986. Dimensions of mainstreaming. *American Annals of the Deaf* 131: 325–30.

A parents' guide to the IEP. 1978. Washington, D.C.: Gallaudet University.

Ramsey, C., and M. Canty. 1994. Inclusion meets education: Can deaf children learn in any classroom? Paper presented at Inclusion? Defining Quality Education for Deaf and Hard of Hearing Students, 26–28 October, at Gallaudet University, Washington, D.C.

Schimmel, D., and L. Fischer. 1987. *Parents, schools, and the law*. Columbia, Md.: The National Committee for Citizens in Education.

Schwartz, S. 1996. *Choices in deafness: A parents' guide*. 2d ed. Kensington, Md.: Woodbine House.

Strong, M. 1995. A review of bilingual/bicultural programs for deaf children in North America. *American Annals of the Deaf* 140(2): 84–94.

U.S. Department of Education. 1980. *Working with schools: A parents' handbook*. Washington, D.C.: Government Printing Office.

HEARING AIDS

Berger, K. W. 1984. *The hearing aid, its operation and development*. 3d ed. Livonia, Mich.: National Hearing Aid Society.

Blatchford, C. 1976. *Yes, I wear a hearing aid*. New York: Lexington School for the Deaf.

Cassie, D. 1976. *The auditory training book*. Danville, Ill.: Interstate Printers and Publishers.

Corliss, E. L. 1981. *Facts about hearing and hearing aids*. Washington, D.C.: U.S. Department of Commerce, National Bureau of Standards.

Gauger, J. S. 1978. *Orientation to hearing aids*. Rochester, N.Y.: National Technical Institute for the Deaf.

The Hearing Journal. [Available from The Laux Company, Inc.; West Bare Hill Road; P.O. Box L; Harvard, MA 01451; (617) 456-8000.]

Simko, C. B. 1986. *Wired for sound: An advanced student workbook on hearing and hearing loss*. Washington, D.C.: Gallaudet University Press.

LANGUAGE DEVELOPMENT

Acredolo, L., and S. Goodwin. 1996. *Baby signs: How to talk with your baby before your baby can talk*. Chicago: Contemporary Books.

Adams, M. J. 1990. *Beginning to read: Thinking and learning about print. A summary*. Urbana-Champaign: University of Illinois Center for the Study of Reading, The Reading Research and Education Center.

ASL in the schools: Policies and curriculum. 1993. Washington, D.C.: Gallaudet University, Continuing Education and Outreach.

Bahan, B., and J. Dannis. 1990. *Signs for me: Basic sign vocabulary for children*. San Diego: DawnSignPress.

Bodner-Johnson, B. 1988. Conversation begins at home. *Perspectives for Teachers of the Hearing Impaired* (November/December): 13–15.

Butterworth, R. R., and M. Flodin. 1991. *Perigee visual dictionary of signing: An A–Z guide to over 1,350 signs of American Sign Language*. New York: Berkeley Publishing Group.

Children's classic videotape sets. San Diego: DawnSignPress.

Cokely, D., and C. Baker-Shenk. 1991. *American sign language: The green books*. Washington, D.C.: Gallaudet University Press.

Collins, H. S. 1993. *Caring for young children: Signing for day care providers and sitters*. Eugene, Ore.: Garlic Press.

———. 1994. *Mother Goose in sign*. Eugene, Ore.: Garlic Press.

Costello, E. 1994. *Random House American Sign Language dictionary*. New York: Random House.

Costello, E., L. G. Lane, and I. B. Pittle. 1979. *Structured tasks for English practice (STEP series)*. Washington, D.C.: Gallaudet College Press.

De Villiers, P., and J. De Villiers. 1979. *Early language*. Cambridge: Harvard University Press.

Durkin, D. 1989. *Teaching them to read*. 5th ed. Boston: Allyn & Bacon.

Eastman, G. L., M. Noretsky, and S. Censoplano. 1989. *From mime to sign*. Silver Spring, Md.: T. J. Publishers.

Fant, L. 1994. *The American Sign Language phrase book*. Rev. ed. Chicago: Contemporary Books, Inc.

Forte, I., and J. Mackenzie. 1989. *The kids stuff book of reading and language arts for the primary grades*. Nashville: Incentive Publications, Inc.

Gibbons, P. 1991. *Learning to learn in a second language*. Portsmouth, N. H.: Heinemann.

Giddan, J. J., and M. Giddan. 1984. *Teaching language with pictures*. Palo Alto, Calif.: Consulting Psychologists Press.

Hafer, J. C., and R. M. Wilson. 1996. *Come sign with us: Sign language activities for children*. 2d ed. Washington, D.C.: Gallaudet University Press.

Hillebrand, L. I., and L. L. Riekehof. 1989. *The joy of signing puzzle book*. Springfield, Mo.: Gospel Publishing House.

Hillerich, R. L. 1986. *The American heritage picture dictionary (gr. K–1)*. Boston: Houghton Mifflin.

Hoemann, H. W. 1986. *Introduction to American Sign Language*. Bowling Green, Ohio: Bowling Green Press.

Kaplan, H., S. J. Bally, and C. Garretson. 1995. *Speechreading: A way to improve understanding*. 2d ed. rev. Washington, D.C.: Gallaudet University Press.

King, C. A., and S. P. Quigley. 1985. *Reading and deafness*. San Diego: College Hill Press.

Larrick, N. 1982. *A parents' guide to children's reading*. 5th ed. Philadelphia: Westminster Press.

Lartz, M. N., and L. J. Lestina. 1995. Strategies deaf mothers use when reading to their young deaf or hard of hearing children. *American Annals of the Deaf* 140: 358–62.

Ling, D., and A. Ling. 1977. *Basic vocabulary language thesaurus for hearing-impaired children*. Washington, D.C.: Alexander Graham Bell Association for the Deaf.

McAnally, P., S. Rose, and S. Quigley. 1994. *Language learning practices with deaf children*. 2d ed. Austin, Tex.: PRO-ED.

Marty, D. R. 1987. *The ear book: A parent's guide to common ear disorders of children*. Jefferson City, Mo.: Lang E.N.T. Publications.

Meier, R. P. 1991. Language acquisition by deaf children. *American Scientist* 79: 60–70.

Miller, A. 1974. *Your child's hearing and speech*. Springfield, Ill.: Charles C. Thomas.

Miller, R., B. Miller, and F. A. Paul. 1989. *Sign language coloring books*. San Diego: DawnSignPress.

O'Rourke, T. J. 1978. *A basic vocabulary: American Sign Language for parents and children*. Silver Spring, Md.: T. J. Publishers.

Padden, C. 1990. The acquisition of fingerspelling by deaf children. In *Theoretical issues in sign language research*, ed. P. Siple and S. D. Fisher, 191–210. Chicago: University of Chicago Press.

The parenting sign video series. 1989. Silver Spring, Md.: Sign Media, Inc. and T. J. Publishers.

Rayner, K., and A. Pollatsek. 1989. *The psychology of reading*. Englewood Cliffs, N.J.: Prentice-Hall.

Ritter-Brinton, K., and D. Stewart. 1992. Hearing parents and deaf children: Some perspectives on sign communication and service delivery. *American Annals of the Deaf* 137: 85–91.

Royster, M. A. n.d. Games and activities for sign language classes. Silver Spring, Md.: National Association of the Deaf.

Rudin, E., and M. Salomon. 1983. *My picture dictionary (gr. 1–3)*. New York: Golden Books.

Russell, D. L. 1994. *Literature for children: A short introduction*. White Plains, N.Y.: Longman.

Schleper, D. R. 1994. *Prereading strategies*. Washington, D.C.: Gallaudet University, Model Secondary School for the Deaf, Department of English.

Sheheen, D. 1984. *A child's picture English-Spanish dictionary (gr. K–6)*. New York: Adama.

Shroyer, E. H. 1988. *Signing English: For parents, teachers, and clinicians*. Greensboro, N. C.: Sugar Sign Press.

Speidel, G. 1987. Conversation and language in the classroom. In *Children's language* (vol. 6), ed. K. E. Nelson. Hillsdale, N.J.: Lawrence Erlbaum Associates.

Sternberg, M. 1994. *American Sign Language dictionary—revised*. New York: HarperCollins.

Swisher, M. V. 1992. The role of parents in developing visual turn-taking in their young deaf children. *American Annals of the Deaf* 137: 92–100.

Verlinde, R., and P. Schragle. 1986. *How to write and caption for Deaf people*. Silver Spring, Md.: T. J. Publishers.

Weaver, C. 1990. *Understanding whole language: From principles to practice*. Portsmouth, N.H.: Heinemann.

———. 1992. The promise of whole language: Education for students with ADHD. *The ChadderBox* 5: 1–7.

Weinstock, J., and C. Erting. 1994. Facilitating ASL and English literacy development in preschool. Paper presented at ASL and English: A Winning Team, 7–9 August, at Greensboro, North Carolina.

Whitehurst, M. W. 1971. *Teaching communication skills to the preschool hearing-impaired child*. Washington, D.C.: Alexander Graham Bell Association for the Deaf.

Wilding-Daez, M. M. 1994. Deaf characters in children's books: How are they perceived? In *Post-Milan: ASL and English literacy: Issues, trends, research*, ed. B. D. Snider. Washington, D.C.: Gallaudet University, Continuing Education and Outreach.

Wischmeyer, L. 1994. Supporting the young bilingual child: Strategies for hearing parents and professionals. Paper presented at ASL and English: A Winning Team, 7–9 August, at Greensboro, North Carolina.

MISCELLANEOUS TOPICS

Ambron, S. 1987. *Child development*. 5th ed. New York: Holt, Rinehart, & Winston.

Anastasiow, N. 1979. Current issues in child development. In *Parent-infant intervention: Communication disorders*, ed. A. Simmons-Martin and D. R. Calvert, 3–12. New York: Grune & Stratton.

Anderson, E. 1991. *Self-esteem for tots to teens*. Wayzata, Minn.: Parent Teaching Publications.

Baum, V. 1981. Counseling families of deaf children. *Journal of the Rehabilitation of the Deaf* 15: 16–19.

Berrett, B., and R. Kelley. 1975. Discipline and the hearing-impaired child. *The Volta Review* 77: 117–24.

Bevan, R. C. 1988. *Hearing-impaired children: A guide for concerned parents and professionals*. Springfield, Ill.: Charles C. Thomas Publishers.

Canter, L., and M. Canter. 1985. *Lee Canter's assertive discipline for parents*. Santa Monica, Calif.: Canter.

Chapman-Weston, D., and M. S. Weston. 1993. *Playful parenting: Turning the dilemma of discipline into fun and games*. New York: Putnam.

Cohen, B. 1980. Emotionally disturbed hearing-impaired children: A review of the literature. *American Annals of the Deaf* 125: 1040–48.

Crary, E. 1990. *Pick up your socks. . . . and other skills growing children need.* Seattle: Parenting Press.

Curwin, R. L., and A. N. Mendler. 1990. *Am I in trouble? Using discipline to teach young children responsibility.* Santa Cruz, Calif.: ETR Associates.

Deafness: A fact sheet. 1990. Washington, D.C.: Gallaudet University, National Information Center on Deafness.

Draper, M. W., and H. E. Draper. 1979. *Caring for children*. Peoria, Ill.: C. A. Bennett.

Erikson, E. H. 1963. *Childhood and society*. 2d ed. New York: Norton.

Ferris, C. 1980. *A hug just isn't enough*. Washington, D.C.: Gallaudet University Press.

Fletcher, L. 1989. *Ben's story: A deaf child's right to sign*. Washington, D.C.: Gallaudet University Press.

Fletcher, R. 1991. *Walking trees*. Portsmouth, N. H.: Heinemann.

Forehand, R., T. Cheney, and P. Yoder. 1974. Parent behavior training: Effects on the non-compliance of a deaf child. *Journal of Behavior Therapy and Experimental Psychiatry* 6: 281–83.

Freeman, R. D., C. F. Carbin, and R. J. Boese. 1981. *Can't your child hear?: A guide for those who care about deaf children.* Austin, Tex.: PRO-ED.

Frishberg, N. 1990. *Interpreting: An introduction*. Rev. ed. Silver Spring, Md.: RID Publications.

*Information for parents: A folio of articles from Perspectives in Education and Deafness.*1990. Washington, D.C.: Gallaudet University, Pre-College Programs.

Garber, S. W., M. D. Garber, and R. F. Spizman. 1987. *Good behavior: Over 2,000 sensible solutions to your child's problems from birth to age twelve*. New York: Villard Books.

Gelfand, D. M., and D. P. Hartmann. 1984. *Child behavior analysis and therapy*. 2d ed. New York: Pergamon Press.

Goodnow, J. J. 1988. Parents' ideas, actions, and feelings: Models and methods for developmental and social psychology. *Child Development* 59: 286–320.

Gordon, I. J. 1979. Parents as teachers—What can they do? In *Parent-infant interventions: Communication disorders*, ed. A. Simmons-Martin and D. R. Calvert, 13–30. New York: Grune & Stratton.

Gordon, T. 1976. *P.E.T. in action*. New York: Wyden Books.

Grant, J. 1987. *The hearing-impaired: Birth to six*. Boston: Little, Brown.

Graziano, A. M., and K. C. Mooney. 1984. *Children and behavior therapy*. New York: Aldine.

Greenberg, J. 1984. *In this sign*. New York: Holt, Rinehart & Winston.

Greene, R. 1993. Hidden factors affecting educational success of ADHD students. *ADHD Report* 1: 8–9.

Griest, D. L., and K. C. Wells. 1983. Behavioral family therapy with conduct disorders in children. *Behavior Therapy* 14: 37–43.

Hall, E. 1982. *Is it catching?: A book for children with hearing-impaired sisters or brothers*. Boulder, Colo.: Ellen Hall.

Harper, R., A. Wiens, and J. Matarazzo. 1978. *Nonverbal communication: The state of the art*. New York: Wiley.

Harrison, R. P. 1974. *Beyond words: An introduction to nonverbal communication*. Englewood Cliffs, N.J.: Prentice-Hall.

Hasenstab, M. S., and J. S. Horner. 1982. *Comprehensive intervention with hearing-impaired infants and preschool children*. Rockville, Md.: Aspen Systems.

Havighurst, R. J. 1972. *Human development and education*. New York: Longman.

Healy, J. M. 1990. *Endangered minds: Why children don't think*. New York: Simon & Schuster.

Helleberg, M. M. 1981. Hearing impairment: A family crisis. *Social Work in Health Care* 5: 33–40.

The House Ear Institute. 1984. *Parent to parent resource catalog*. Los Angeles: The House Ear Institute.

Kaye, P. 1991. *Games for learning: Ten minutes a day to help your child do well in school—from kindergarten to third grade*. New York: Farrar, Straus & Giroux.

Kazdin, A. E., T. C. Siegel, and D. Bass. 1992. Cognitive problem-solving skills training and parent management training in the treatment of antisocial behavior in children. *Journal of Consulting and Clinical Psychology* 60: 733–47.

Kisor, H. 1990. *What's that pig outdoors: A memoir of deafness*. New York: Hill & Wang.

Kozoloff, M. A. 1979. *A program for families of children with learning and behavior problems*. New York: Wiley.

Krumboltz, J. D., and C. E. Thoresen, eds. 1976. *Counseling methods*. New York: Holt, Rinehart & Winston.

Kubler-Ross, E. 1969. *On death and dying*. New York: Macmillan.

Lane, H. 1988. Is there a "psychology of the deaf"? *Exceptional Children* 55: 7–19.

———. 1994. The cochlear implant controversy. *World Federation of the Deaf News*, 2–3.

Lillie, D., P. L. Trohanis, and K. W. Goin, eds. 1976. *Teaching parents to teach!: A guide to working with the special child*. New York: Walker.

Luterman, D. 1979. *Counseling parents of hearing-impaired children*. Boston: Little, Brown.

Mace, A., K. Wallace, M. Whan, and P. Stelmachoica. 1991. Relevant factors in the identification of hearing loss. *Ear and Hearing* 12: 287–93.

Martin, D. S., ed. 1991. *Advances in cognition, education, and deafness*. Washington, D.C.: Gallaudet University Press.

Maxon, A. B., and D. L. Bracket. 1992. *The hearing-impaired child: Infancy through high school years*. Boston: Andover Medical Publishers.

McCormick, B. 1975. Parent guidance: The needs of families and of the professional worker. *The Teacher of the Deaf* 73: 315–30.

Medwid, D., and D. Chapman-Weston. 1996. *Kid-friendly parenting*. Washington, D.C.: Gallaudet University Press.

Morris, D., P. Collett, P. Marsh, and M. O'Shaughnessy. 1979. *Gestures*. New York: Stein & Day.

Murphy, A. T. 1979. The families of handicapped children: Context for disability. *The Volta Review* 5: 265–78.

National Directory of TTY numbers. 1995. Washington, D.C.: Telecommunications for the Deaf.

Navarra, T. 1993. *On my own: Helping kids help themselves*. Monroe, Wash.: Barron.

Neyhos, A. I., and G. E. Austin. 1978. *Deafness and adolescence*. Washington, D.C.: Alexander Graham Bell Association for the Deaf.

O'Dell, S. 1974. Training parents in behavior modification: A review. *Psychological Bulletin* 81: 418–33.

Pahz, J., and C. Pahz. 1977. *Will love be enough? A deaf child in the family*. Silver Spring, Md.: National Association of the Deaf.

Peterson, J. W. 1977. *I have a sister—My sister is deaf*. New York: Harper & Row.

Phelan, T. 1985. *1-2-3 magic: Training your preschoolers and preteens to do what you want*. Glen Ellyn, Ill.: Child Management Press.

Pollock, P. 1982. *Keeping it secret*. New York: Putnam.

Raffini, J. P. 1980. *Discipline: Negotiating conflicts with today's kids*. Englewood Cliffs, N.J.: Prentice-Hall.

Raimondo, B. 1994. A hearing parents' perspective on raising a deaf child. Paper presented at French-American Conference on Bilingual Education, 20 April, Kendall Demonstration Elementary School, Washington, D.C.

Riskind, M. 1981. *Apple is my sign*. Boston: Houghton Mifflin.

Ross, A. O. 1981. *Child behavior therapy: Principles, procedures and empirical basis*. New York: Wiley.

Sabatino, D. A., A. C. Sabatino, and L. Mann, eds. 1983. *Discipline and behavior: A handbook of tactics, strategies, and programs*. Rockville, Md.: Aspen Systems.

Schildroth, A., and M. Karchmer. 1986. *Deaf children in America*. San Diego: College Hill Press.

Schmaman, F. D., and G. Straker. 1980. Counseling parents of the hearing-impaired child during the post-diagnostic period. *Language, Speech, and Hearing Services in the Schools* 11: 251–59.

Seligman, M. 1991. Grandparents of disabled grandchildren: Hopes, fears and adaptation. *Families in Society: The Journal of Contemporary Human Services* (March): 147–152.

Shontz, F. C. 1965. Reaction to crisis. *The Volta Review* 67: 364–70.

Shulman, B. B., ed. 1995. Educating students who are deaf and hard of hearing: Challenges 2000 [Special Issue]. *Journal of Childhood Communication Disorders* 17 (1).

Spencer, P., B. Bodner-Johnson, and M. Gutfreund. 1992. Interacting with infants with a hearing loss: What can we learn from mothers who are deaf? *Journal of Early Intervention* 16: 64–78.

Spitzer, A., C. Webster-Stratton, and T. Hollinsworth. 1991. Coping with conduct problem children: Parents gaining knowledge and control. *Journal of Child Clinical Psychology* 20: 413–27.

Spradley, T. S., and J. P. Spradley. 1985. *Deaf like me*. Washington, D.C.: Gallaudet University Press.

Stein, L. K., E. D. Mindel, and T. Jabaley. 1981. *Deafness and mental health*. New York: Grune & Stratton.

Toby, E., and S. Hastenstaub. 1991. Effects of a nucleus multi-channel cochlear implant upon speech production of children. *Ear and Hearing* 12(4) [Supplement].

Tucker, P. T. 1986. Interpreter services: Legal rights of hearing-impaired persons. In *Oral interpreting: Principles and practices*, ed. W. H. Northcott. Baltimore, Md.: University Park Press.

Vygotsky, L. 1978. *Mind in society: The development of higher psychological processes*. Cambridge: Harvard University Press.

Wadsworth, B. J. 1971. *Piaget's theory of cognitive development: An introduction for students of psychology and education*. New York: David McKay.

Webber, J., and B. Scheuermann. 1991. Accentuate the positive.... eliminate the negative! *Teaching Exceptional Children* (Fall): 13–19.

Webster, L. M., and W. B. Green. 1973. Behavior modification in the deaf classroom: Current applications and suggested alternatives. *American Annals of the Deaf* 118: 511–18.

Webster-Stratton, C. 1991. *The dinosaur videotape curriculum for young children: Therapist manual and videotapes*. Seattle: Seth Enterprises.

————. 1992. *The incredible years: A trouble-shooting guide for parents of children aged 3 to 8 years old*. Toronto: Umbrella Press.

————. 1992. *The parents and children videotape series: Programs 1–10*. Seattle: Seth Enterprises.

Zawolkow, E. G., and S. Defiore. 1986. Educational interpreting for elementary and secondary-level hearing-impaired students. *American Annals of the Deaf* 131: 26–32.

References

Adams, J. W. 1995. Behavior problems of deaf and hard-of-hearing children: A cause for assessment? Paper presented at the Eighteenth International Congress on Education of the Deaf, July, Tel Aviv, Israel.

Adams, J. W., and R. Tidwell. 1989. An instructional guide for reducing the stress of hearing parents of hearing-impaired children. *American Annals of the Deaf* 134: 323–28.

Algozzine, R., R. Schmid, and D. C. Mercer. 1981. *Childhood behavior disorders: Applied research and educational practice*. Rockville, Md.: Aspen Systems.

Allen, J. C., and M. L. Allen. 1979. Discovering and accepting hearing-impairment: Initial reactions of parents. *The Volta Review* 81(5): 279–85.

Andersen, C., J. Bergan, B. Landish, and N. Lewis. 1985. *Communication in human relationships*. Washington, D.C.: Gallaudet University.

Andreozzi, L. L. 1996. *Child-centered family therapy*. New York: Wiley.

Arieff, I. 1991. Deaf babies can "babble" with hands. *Buffalo News*.

Axelsson, M. 1994. Second language acquisition. In *Bilingualism in deaf education*, ed. I. Ahlgren and K. Hyltestam. International Studies on Sign Language and Communication of the Deaf, vol. 27. Hamburg, Germany: Signum Press.

Baker, B. L., A. J. Brightman, L. J. Heifetz, and D. M. Murphy. 1976. *Behavior problems*. Champaign, Ill.: Research Press.

Beck, R. L. 1991. The forgotten family. *SHHH Journal* 12: 7–9.

Becker, S. 1981. Counseling the families of deaf children: A mental health worker speaks out. *Journal of Rehabilitation of the Deaf* 15:10–15.

Belcastro, F. 1979. Use of behavior modification with hearing-impaired subjects. *American Annals of the Deaf* 124: 820–23.

Benderly, B. L. 1990. *Dancing without music.* Washington D. C.: Gallaudet University Press.

Bienvenu, M. J. 1991. Perspectives on the word "deafness." *The BiCultural Center News* 35:8.

Bodner-Johnson, B. 1988. Conversation begins at home—around the table. *Perspectives for Teachers of the Hearing Impaired* 7(2): 13–15.

———. 1991. Family conversation style: Its effects on the deaf child's participation. *Exceptional Children* 57(6): 502–8.

Body language. 1995. *Dateline NBC.* New York: National Broadcasting Company.

Bolton, B. 1976. *Psychology of deafness for rehabilitation counselors.* Baltimore, Md.: University Park Press.

Boothroyd, A. 1982. *Hearing-impairments in young children.* Englewood Cliffs, N.J.: Prentice-Hall.

Bragg, B. 1994. Culture, language, and deafness (collectivism or individualism). In *Deafness: Life and culture: A Deaf American monograph*, ed. M. D. Garretson, 15–16. Silver Spring, Md.: National Association of the Deaf.

Bravin, J. A. and Bravin, P. W. 1992. Communication and deaf children: A common sense approach. In *Viewpoints on deafness: A Deaf American monograph*, ed. M. D. Garretson, 35–37. Silver Spring, Md.: National Association of the Deaf.

Brenner, B. 1983. *Love and discipline.* New York: Ballantine Books.

Broesterhuizen, M. 1990. The prediction of social-emotional problems in deaf children. Paper presented at the Seventeenth Inter-

national Congress on Education of the Deaf, July–August, Rochester, New York.

Brown, S. C. 1986. Etiological trends, characteristics, and distribu-
tions. In *Deaf children in America*, ed. A. N. Schildroth and M. A.
Karchmer, 33–54. San Diego: College Hill Press.

Calderon, R., and M. T. Greenberg. 1993. Considerations in the adaptation of families with school-aged deaf children. In *Psychological
perspectives on deafness*, ed. M. Marschark and M. Clark. Hillsdale, N.J.: Lawrence Erlbaum Associates.

Canter, L., and M. Canter. 1985. *Lee Canter's assertive discipline for
parents*. Rev. ed. Santa Monica, Calif.: Canter.

Cavanagh, M. E. 1990. *The counseling experience: A theoretical and
practical approach*. Prospect Heights, Ill.: Waveland Press.

Champ-Wilson, A. 1982. Successful parenting: Fact or fiction. In *Parent education resource manual*, 191–96. Washington, D.C.: Gallaudet College, Division of Public Services.

Christensen, K. 1990. American sign language and English: Parallel
bilingualism. In *Communication issues among Deaf people: A Deaf
American monograph*, ed. M. D. Garretson, 27–30. Silver Spring,
Md.: National Association of the Deaf.

Cohen, J. 1990. Total communication: A parent's perspective. In *Communication issues among Deaf people: A Deaf American monograph*, ed. M. D. Garretson, 31–34. Silver Spring, Md.: National
Association of the Deaf.

Colon, A. 1996. Speaking the language of the Deaf culture. *Buffalo
News*, A7–A8.

Conference of Executives of American Schools for the Deaf. 1976.
Total communication definition adopted. *American Annals of the
Deaf* 121: 358.

Connard, P., and R. Kantor. 1988. A partnership perspective viewing
normal-hearing parent/hearing-impaired child communication.
The Volta Review 90: 133–48.

Correspondence course for parents of young deaf children. 1983. Los Angeles: John Tracy Clinic.

Davis, F. 1973. *Inside intuition: What we know about nonverbal communication*. New York: McGraw-Hill.

Davis, J. 1986. Academic placement in perspective. In *Deafness in perspective*, ed. D. M. Luterman, 205–24. San Diego: College Hill Press.

Deyo, D., and L. Gelzer. 1991. *When a hearing loss is diagnosed*. Washington, D.C.: Gallaudet University, National Information Center on Deafness.

Dinkmeyer, D., and G. D. McKay. 1989. *The parents' handbook: Systematic training for effective parenting (STEP)*. 3d ed. Circle Pines, Minn.: American Guidance Service.

Dixon, S. D., and M. T. Stein. 1992. *Encounters with children: Pediatric behavior and development*. 2d ed. St. Louis, Mo.: Mosby Year Book.

Dolnick, E. 1993. Deafness as culture. *The Atlantic Monthly* (September): 37–53.

Drasgow, E. 1992. Bilingual/bicultural deaf education: An overview. *Sign Language Studies* 80:243–65.

———. 1995. Pathway to linguistic competence: Rationale for American Sign Language as the first sign language of deaf children. Typescript.

Epstein, S. 1987. A medical approach to hearing loss. In *Choices in deafness: A parents' guide*, ed. S. Schwartz, 1–14. Kensington, Md.: Woodbine House.

Erting, C. J. 1987. Cultural conflict in a school for deaf children. In *Understanding deafness socially*, ed. P. L. Higgins and J. E. Nash, 129–50. Springfield, Ill.: Charles C. Thomas.

Firth, A. L. 1994. The Americans with Disabilities Act: Where are we now? In *Deafness: Life and culture: A Deaf American monograph*, ed. M. D. Garretson, 41–44. Silver Spring, Md.: National Association of the Deaf.

Forehand, R. L., and R. J. McMahon. 1981. *Helping the noncompliant child: A clinician's guide to parent training*. New York: Guilford Press.

Frick, P. J. 1993. Childhood conduct problems in a family context. *School Psychology Review* 22: 376–85.

Garbarino, J. 1992. *Children and families in the social environment*. 2d ed. New York: Aldine De Gruyter.

Gatty, J. 1987. The oral approach: A professional point of view. In *Choices in deafness: A parents' guide*, ed. S. Schwartz, 57–64. Kensington, Md.: Woodbine House.

Gelfand, D. M., and D. P. Hartmann. 1984. *Child behavior analysis and therapy*. 2d ed. New York: Pergamon Press.

Gesell, A., F. L. Ilg, and L. Bates-Ames. 1977. *The child from five to ten*. Rev. ed. New York: Harper & Row.

Goldberg, B. 1995. Families facing choices. *ASHA* (May): 39–47.

Goldberg, H. K. 1979. Hearing-impairment: A family crisis. *Social Work in Health Care* 5: 33–40.

Goldstein, S. 1995. *Understanding and managing children's classroom behavior*. New York: Wiley.

Goodstein, H. 1990. American Sign Language. In *Communication issues among Deaf people: A Deaf American monograph*, ed. M. D. Garretson, 47–49. Silver Spring, Md.: National Association of the Deaf.

Grant, J. 1987. *The hearing impaired: Birth to six*. Boston: Little, Brown.

Green, R. R. 1971. Pointers for parents: The hearing-impaired child at home. *Highlights* (Winter) 5–7.

Greenberg, M. T. 1990. *Family communication and deaf children's self-esteem*. Keynote address presented at the Twelfth Biennial Convention of the American Society for Deaf Children, Vancouver, British Columbia.

Gregory, S. 1976. *The deaf child and his family*. New York: Wiley.

Groce, N. 1985. *Everyone here spoke sign language: Hereditary deafness on Martha's Vineyard*. Cambridge: Harvard University Press.

Hafer, J. C., and E. Ditman-Richard. 1990. What hearing parents should learn about Deaf culture. In *Information for parents: A folio of articles from Perspectives in Education and Deafness*, 15–17. Washington, D.C.: Gallaudet University, Pre-College Programs.

Hardman, M. L., C. J. Drew, and M. W. Egan. 1990. *Human exceptionality: Society, school, and family*. Boston: Allyn & Bacon.

Hawkins, L., and S. Baker-Hawkins. 1990. Perspectives on deafness: Hearing parents of deaf children. In *Communication issues among Deaf people: A Deaf American monograph*, ed. M. D. Garretson, 63–65. Silver Spring, Md.: National Association of the Deaf.

Heimgartner, N. L. 1982. *Behavioral traits of deaf children*. Springfield, Ill.: Charles C. Thomas.

Henderson, D., and A. Hendershott. 1992. ASL and the family system. *American Annals of the Deaf* 136: 325–29.

Henggeler, S. W., S. M. Watson, J. P. Whelan, and M. A. Malone. 1990. The adaptation of hearing parents of hearing-impaired youth. *American Annals of the Deaf* 135: 211–16.

Herbert, M. 1981. *Behavioral treatment of problem children: A practice manual*. New York: Grune & Stratton.

Higgins, P. L., and J. E. Nash. 1987. *Understanding deafness socially*. Springfield, Ill.: Charles C. Thomas.

Hubler, S., ed. 1983. *When your perfect child is deaf.* (A discussion guide to accompany the film: "My perfect child is deaf.") Los Angeles: The House Ear Institute.

Jackendoff, R. 1994. *Patterns in the mind: Language and human nature.* New York: BasicBooks.

Jamieson, J. R. 1994. Teaching as transaction: Vygotskian perspectives on deafness and mother-child interaction. *Exceptional Children* 60: 434–49.

Jordan, I. K. 1992. Language and change. In *Viewpoints on deafness: A Deaf American Monograph,* ed. M. D. Garretson, 69–71. Silver Spring, Md.: National Association of the Deaf.

Kampfe, C. M. 1989. Parental reaction to a child's hearing impairment. *American Annals of the Deaf* 134: 255–59.

Kannapell, B. 1993. *Language choice—identity choice.* Burtonsville, Md.: Linstok Press.

Kazdin, A. E. 1984. *Behavior modification in applied settings.* 5th ed. Pacific Grove, Calif.: Brooks/Cole Publishing.

Kipila, E., and B. Williams-Scott. 1990. Cued Speech: A response to "Controversy within sign language." In *Communication issues among Deaf people: A Deaf American Monograph,* ed. M. D. Garretson, 71–74. Silver Spring, Md.: National Association of the Deaf.

Kluwin, T. N., and M. G. Gaustad. 1992. Predicting family communication choices. *American Annals of the Deaf* 136: 28–34.

Kretschmer, R. R., ed. 1979. Parenting a hearing-impaired child: An interview with Ken Moses. *The Volta Review* 81: 73–80.

Kretschmer, R. R., and L. Kretschmer. 1986. Language in perspective. In *Deafness in perspective,* ed. D. M. Luterman, 131–66. San Diego: College Hill Press.

Lane, H. 1989. *When the mind hears: A history of the Deaf.* New York: Vintage Books.

————. 1994. The cochlear implant controversy. *World Federation of the Deaf News*: 2–3.

Lane, H., R. Hoffmeister, and B. Bahan. 1996. *A journey into the deaf-world*. San Diego: DawnSignPress.

Lederberg, A. R. 1993. The impact of deafness on mother-child and peer relationships. In *Psychological perspectives in deafness*, ed. M. Marschark and M. Clark, 93–119. Hillsdale, N.J.: Lawrence Erlbaum Associates.

Liben, L. S. 1978. *Deaf children: Developmental perspectives*. New York: Academic Press.

Ling, D. 1984. *Early intervention for hearing-impaired children: Total communication options*. San Diego: College Hill Press.

Luterman, D. M. 1986. *Deafness in perspective*. San Diego: College Hill Press.

Madsen, C. K., and C. H. Madsen. 1972. *Parents/children/discipline: A positive approach*. Boston: Allyn & Bacon.

Mahshie, S. N. 1995. *Educating deaf children bilingually*. Washington, D.C.: Gallaudet University, Pre-College Programs.

Malcolm, R. J. 1990. My sister is deaf and what about me? . . . Meeting the needs of siblings. *Perspectives in Education and Deafness* 9: 12–14.

Marschark, M., and M. D. Clark, eds. 1993. *Psychological perspectives on deafness*. Hillsdale, N.J.: Lawrence Erlbaum Associates.

Mather, S. M. 1990. Home and classroom communication. In *Educational and developmental aspects of deafness*, ed. D. F. Moores and K. P. Meadow-Orlans, 232–54. Washington, D.C.: Gallaudet University Press.

Matthews, T. J., and C. F. Reich. 1993. Constraints on communication in classrooms for the deaf. *American Annals of the Deaf* 138: 14–18.

McArthur, S. H. 1982. *Raising your hearing-impaired child: A guideline for parents*. Washington, D.C.: Alexander Graham Bell Association for the Deaf.

McConnell, L. 1996. Mothers and babies. *Preview* (Winter): 5–7.

Meador, H. E. 1994. The "how" of a language. In *Deafness: Life and culture: A Deaf American monograph*, ed. M. D. Garretson, 81–84. Silver Spring, Md.: National Association of the Deaf.

Meadow, K. P. 1968. Parental responses to the medical ambiguities of deafness. *Journal of Health and Social Behavior* 9: 299–309.

———. 1980. *Deafness and child development*. Berkeley: University of California Press.

———. 1995. Sources of stress for mothers and fathers of deaf and hard-of-hearing infants. *American Annals of the Deaf* 140: 352–57.

Medwid, D., and Chapman-Weston, D. 1996. *Kid-friendly parenting*. Washington, D.C.: Gallaudet University Press.

Mertens, D. M. 1989. Social experiences of hearing-impaired high school youth. *American Annals of the Deaf* 134: 15–19.

Mindel, E. D., and V. Feldman. 1987. The impact of deaf children on their families. In *They grow in silence: Understanding deaf children and adults*, 2d ed., ed. E. D. Mindel and M. Vernon, 1–29. San Diego: College Hill Press.

Mindel, E. D., and M. Vernon. 1987. *They grow in silence: Understanding deaf children and adults*. 2d ed. San Diego: College Hill Press.

Mira, M. 1972. Behavior modification applied to training young deaf children. *Exceptional Children* 39: 225–29.

Moores, D. F. 1987. *Educating the deaf: Psychology, principles, and practices*. 3d ed. Boston: Houghton Mifflin.

Moses, K. L. 1985. Infant deafness and parental grief: Psychosocial early intervention. In *Educating the hearing-impaired child*, ed.

F. Powell, T. Finitzo-Hieber, S. Friel-Patti, and D. Henderson, 86–102. San Diego: College Hill Press.

Murphy, A. T. 1979. The families of handicapped children: Context for disability. *The Volta Review* 81: 265–78.

Naiman, D. W., and J. D. Schein. 1978. *For parents of deaf children*. Silver Spring, Md.: National Association of the Deaf.

Newman, L. R. 1992. The bilingual and bicultural approach. In *Viewpoints on deafness: A Deaf American monograph*, ed. M. D. Garretson, 92–95. Silver Spring, Md.: National Association of the Deaf.

Nowell, R. C., and L. E. Marshak, eds. 1994. *Understanding deafness and the rehabilitation process*. Boston: Allyn & Bacon.

Ogden, P. 1984. Parenting in the mainstream. *The Volta Review* 86: 29–39.

———. 1996. *The silent garden: Raising your deaf child*. Washington, D.C.: Gallaudet University Press.

Okwara, M. G. 1994. Discovering my identity and culture. In *Deafness: Life and culture: A Deaf American monograph*, ed. M. D. Garretson, 85–87. Silver Spring, Md.: National Association of the Deaf.

Padden, C. 1980. The Deaf community and the culture of Deaf people. In *Sign language and the Deaf community*, ed. C. Baker and R. Battison. Silver Spring, Md.: National Association of the Deaf.

Padden, C., and T. Humphries. 1988. *Deaf in America: Voices from a culture*. Cambridge: Harvard University Press.

Paget, S. 1983. Long-term grieving in parents of hearing-impaired children: A synthesis of parental experience. *Journal of the British Association of the Teachers of the Deaf* 3: 78–82.

Parreca, D. 1987. An audiological overview. In *Choices in deafness: A parents' guide*, ed. S. Schwartz, 15–22. Kensington, Md.: Woodbine House.

Paul, P. V., and D. W. Jackson. 1993. *Toward a psychology of deafness: Theoretical and empirical perspectives*. Boston: Allyn & Bacon.

Paul, P. V., and S. Quigley. 1990. *Education and deafness*. White Plains, N.Y.: Longman.

Peeks, B. 1992. Protection and social context: Understanding a child's problem behavior. *Elementary School Guidance and Counseling* 26: 295–304.

Peterson, L. C. 1982. The child as a person. In *Parent education resource manual*, 171–76. Washington, D.C.: Gallaudet College, Division of Public Services.

Pettit, G. S., J. E. Bates, and K. A. Dodge. 1993. Family interaction patterns and children's conduct problems at home and school: A longitudinal perspective. *School Psychology Review* 22: 403–20.

Plapinger, D., and R. Kretschmer. 1991. The effect of context on the interactions between a normally-hearing mother and her hearing-impaired child. *The Volta Review* 93: 75–87.

Poor, G. S. 1992. Early ASL training for hearing families with deaf children. In *Viewpoints on deafness: A Deaf American monograph*, ed. M. D. Garretson, 109–111. Silver Spring, Md.: National Association of the Deaf.

Proctor, A. 1983. Early home intervention for hearing-impaired infants and their parents. *The Volta Review* 86: 150–55.

Quigley, S. P., and R. E. Kretschmer. 1982. *The education of deaf children: Issues, theory, and practice*. Baltimore, Md.: University Park Press.

Radetsky, P. 1994. Silence, signs, and wonder. *Discover* (August): 60–68.

Rhode G., W. R. Jenson, H. K. Reavis. 1992. *The tough kid book: Practical classroom management strategies*. Longmont, Colo.: Sopris West.

Ritter-Brinton, K., and Stewart, D. 1992. Hearing parents and deaf children: Some perspectives on sign communication and service delivery. *American Annals of the Deaf* 137: 85–91.

Rodda, M., and C. Grove. 1987. *Language, cognition and deafness*. Hillsdale, N.J.: Lawrence Erlbaum Associates.

Rosen, R. 1986. Deafness: A social perspective. In *Deafness in perspective*, ed. D. M. Luterman. San Diego: College Hill Press.

Ruben, B. D. 1984. *Communication and human behavior*. New York: Macmillan.

Ryan, E. 1992. A deaf child in the family: New reasons to hope? *Perspectives in Education and Deafness* 11: 14–17.

Scheetz, N. A. 1993. *Orientation to deafness*. Boston: Allyn & Bacon.

Schick, B., and E. Gale. 1995. Preschool deaf and hard-of-hearing students' interactions during ASL and English storytelling. *American Annals of the Deaf* 140: 363–70.

Schildroth, A. N., and S. A. Hotto. 1996. Changes in student characteristics and program characteristics, 1984–85 and 1994–95. *American Annals of the Deaf* 141: 68–71.

Schlesinger, H. S. 1985. Deafness, mental health, and language. In *Education of the hearing-impaired child*, ed. F. Powell, T. Finitzo-Hieber, S. Friel-Patti, and D. Henderson, 103–13. San Diego: College Hill Press.

Schlesinger, H. S., and K. P. Meadow. 1972. *Sound and sign: Childhood deafness and mental health*. Berkeley: University of California Press.

Schragle, P. S., and G. Bateman. 1994. Impact of captioning. In *Deafness: Life and culture: A Deaf American monograph*, ed. M. D. Garretson, 101–4. Silver Spring, Md.: National Association of the Deaf.

Schwartz, S., ed. 1987. *Choices in deafness: A parents' guide*. Kensington, Md.: Woodbine House.

————. 1996. *Choices in deafness: A parents' guide to communication options.* 2d ed. Bethesda, Md.: Woodbine House.

Sevigny-Skyer, S. 1990. Personally speaking. *Journal of Counseling and Development* 68: 336–37.

Sloman, L., A. Perry, and F. Frankenburg. 1987. Family therapy with deaf member families. *American Journal of Family Therapy* 15: 242–52.

Stinson, M. S. 1991. Affective and social development. In *Understanding deafness and the rehabilitation process*, ed. R. Nowell and L. Marshak. Needham Heights, Mass.: Allyn & Bacon.

Swisher, M. V. 1992. Conversational interaction between deaf children and their hearing mothers: The role of visual attention. In *Theoretical issues in sign language research*, ed. P. Siple and S. D. Fischer, 111–34. Chicago: University of Chicago Press.

Today. 1996, August 9. New York: National Broadcasting Company.

Tranchin, R., and B. Bragg. 1994. Correspondence between a hearing father and a deaf adult. In *Deafness: Life and culture: A Deaf American monograph*, ed. M. D. Garretson, 117–20. Silver Spring, Md.: National Association of the Deaf.

Trychin, S. 1990. You, me, and hearing loss makes three. *SHHH Journal* 11: 7–11.

Vernon, M., and J. F. Andrews. 1990. *The psychology of deafness*. New York: Longman.

Vernon, M., and B. Daigle. 1994. Bilingual and bicultural education. In *Deafness: Life and culture: A Deaf American monograph*, ed. M. D. Garretson, 121–26. Silver Spring, Md.: National Association of the Deaf.

Walters, R. P. 1989. Nonverbal communication in group counseling. In *Group counseling: A developmental approach*, 3d ed., ed. G. M. Gazda, 203–33. Boston: Allyn & Bacon.

Warren, C., and S. Hasenstab. 1986. Self concept of severely to profoundly hearing-impaired children. *The Volta Review* 88: 289–95.

Watson, S. M., S. W. Henggeler, and J. P. Whelan. 1990. Family functioning and the social adaptation of hearing-impaired youths. *Journal of Abnormal Child Psychology* 18: 143–63.

Webster-Stratton, C. 1993. Strategies for helping early school-aged children with oppositional defiant and conduct disorders: The importance of home-school partnerships. *School Psychology Review* 22: 437–57.

Webster-Stratton, C., and M. Herbert. 1994. *Troubled families—problem children: Working with parents: A collaborative process*. New York: Wiley.

Weiss, M. 1994. Strengthening the center line: Family factors that influence social/emotional, communication and educational development. Paper presented at the Kansas School for the Deaf Family, Fun and Facts Parent Weekend, Olathe, Kansas.

Winslow, J. 1994, April. Personal correspondence. Kansas School for the Deaf Family, Fun and Facts Parent Weekend, Olathe, Kansas.

Woodcock, K. 1992. Cochlear implants vs. Deaf culture? In *Viewpoints on deafness: A Deaf American monograph*, ed. M. D. Garretson, 151–55. Silver Spring, Md.: National Association of the Deaf.

Index